ETHIOPIA'S REVOLUTION

ETHIOPIA'S REVOLUTION

By Raúl Valdéz Vivó

INTERNATIONAL PUBLISHERS
New York

Originally published in 1977 as *Etiopia, la revolución
    desconocida* by Editorial de Cienias Sociales
Translation © 1978 by International Publishers Co., Inc.
First edition, 1978
Printed in the United States of America

Library of Congress Cataloging in Publication Data

Valdés Vivó, Rául.
    Ethiopia's revolution.

    Translation of Etiopia: la revolución desconocida.
    1. Ethiopia—History—Revolution, 1974. I. Title.
DT387.95.V3413   963'.06   78-16988
ISBN 0-7178-0556-5 pbk.

In Ethiopia they have adopted very radical measures. In a feudal country where the peasants were slaves, they nationalized the land and distributed it among the peasants. They carried out an urban reform, allowing only one house to a family. They organized a powerful movement in the cities, a form of organization they called the *kebele*. That is, they organized the families in the poor urban areas. They nationalized the principal industries of the country, revolutionized the armed forces, politicized the soldiers, created Political Committees.

Although the Ethiopian Revolution faces powerful enemies, the people are determined to fight, for no true revolution can easily be defeated. We believe that the success and consolidation of the Ethiopian Revolution have enormous importance for Africa.

FIDEL CASTRO
March, 1977

Contents

Foreword

THE NEWEST and a most thoroughgoing revolution has taken place in the oldest country in the world: Ethiopia. In three days a three thousand year old monarchy was toppled. This revolution has propelled aged Ethiopia from a society of oppressive feudal-bourgois backwardness into the orbit of socialist countries with rocketlike speed.

Raúl Valdés Vivó has written about this and more: The revolution, its beginnings, its victory over the Haile Selassie regime on a September morn in 1974; and its confrontations with recurrent waves of counterrevolution. He tells how the workers and peasants took its banner to their hearts and arms to their hands to defend the revolution and carry it forward to accomplish unprecedented radical agrarian and urban social reforms, nationalization of industry, banking and commerce, and the conversion of urban properties into public ownership. Valdés Vivó describes how the revolution smashed caste-privileges and national exclusiveness, and opened the way to the democratization, organization, and politicalization of the popular masses of civilians and soldiers alike; and how it is addressing the widespread problems of poverty, illiteracy, disease, prejudice, etc.

Raúl Valdés Vivó shows us the steps the revolutionary process has taken which brought it to its logical connection with the true ideology of modern social revolution—Marxism-Leninism. He discloses how the complex problems of leadership contributed to and in turn found basic solution in the emergence of an outstanding revolutionary talent—Lieutenant Colonel Mengistu Haile Mariam, Socialist Ethiopia's brilliant leader and builder of its Marxist-Leninist vanguard party.

Frederick Douglass, the great 19th century anti-slavery liberator, appealing to his youthful readers to join with Maceo's rising for the liberation of Cuba from the Spanish yoke, invoked the great principle of internationalism, of the common bonds that unite the victims of tyranny against a common oppressor. "A blow struck for freedom anywhere, is a blow for freedom everywhere," Douglass wrote. As it was with Cuba, so it is with Ethiopia. The victory of the Ethiopian Revolution will most favorably influence the relation of forces on the African continent. It is a mighty blow to colonialism, neo-colonialism and imperialism in general and will constitute a great inspiration and source of support to the peoples of Southern Africa in battle for their national liberation.

Ethiopia is the situs of the biblical land of ancient Abyssinia, of King Solomon and the Queen of Sheba, and figures prominently in the religious and ethnic points of reference of the thirty million Afro-Americans of the United States. The Ethiopian Revolution will hold a special interest for the Black people who still suffer all manner of discrimination and racial prejudice. Its message, that the path of socialism is the only true way to social progress in our times, will stir the hopes and militancy of peoples of color who suffer the experiences of racist indignities and national oppression.

U.S. imperialism was supportive in every way to Haile Selassie's backward repressive regime. It counted upon manipulating the prestige of this oldest of states in its design for neo-colonialist domination in an Africa where the old-style colonialism could no longer be maintained by imperialism. It hoped to

divert the anti-monarchy upsurge into safe channels
by virtue of U.S. influence in the higher echelons of
the military and the government bureaucracy—having
provided the training for their top cadres. Disappointed
in realizing these expectations, U.S.
imperialism put its considerable resources at the
service of counterrevolution in Ethiopia. It inspired
attempts at coups, assassinations of leaders, the organization
of subsidies—military and financial—to
secessionist provincial nationalist movements. It
conspired with Siad Barre and pledged support and
material aid to the Somali expansionist adventure.
The armed forces of Somalia drove 700 km. into the
Ogaden Province of Ethiopia before they were finally
stopped and routed by the armed forces and peoples
militia of revolutionary Ethiopia. The ability of the
Ethiopian Revolution to meet the treacherous invasion
from Somalia was greatly aided by the heroic
measures undertaken to render necessary material
support to its defense effort by its allies—the Soviet
Union, Cuba, the Peoples Republic of Yemen, and
other socialist lands, as well as Kenya and other
front-line countries.

The leader of the revolutionary forces of Ethiopia—
Lieutenant Colonel Mengistu Haile Mariam—has
said that:

> We have emerged triumphant in the Ogaden
> war waged against the reactionary Somali ruling
> class, and although we're marching along
> the correct path, the long and bloody struggle of
> the Ethiopian masses has still a long way to go.
> Imperialism and Arab reaction are now guiding
> and fully supporting the secessionist rebellions
> (of Eritrean groups) in the North.

Mengistu expresses confidence that the forces of
justice, peace and progress the world over will arise
to the support of the just cause of the Ethiopian Revolution.

John Reed's book, *Ten Days That Shook The World,* was a volume of reportage that gave millions an on-the-scene acquaintance with the event that ushered in a new epoch in human history—the October Revolution. Raúl Valdés Vivó, in his *Ethiopia's Revolution,* has written a wonderful, insightful sequel to the latest (but by no means the last) offspring of that pioneer of modern revolutions—Great October. It deserves to reach the hands, hearts and minds of the millions.

James E. Jackson

ETHIOPIA'S REVOLUTION

1 The Emperor Is Arrested

I

AT 8:00 A.M. on September 12, 1974—Maskaram 2, 1967, or September 2, 1967, in the Ethiopian calendar, according to which the days are only 12 hours long (as long as there is daylight, that is)—a small white Volkswagen raced through the vast gardens of tall eucalyptus trees and gigantic rare flowers (the ones that cluster on a single stem and are sometimes many different shades of red and yellow) and stopped short at the main entrance to the Imperial Palace of Addis Ababa. Very few people knew that the occupants of the car were about to arrest Emperor Haile Selassie I, King of Kings, the Chosen One of God, Lion of Judah, direct descendant of the Queen of Sheba and King Solomon.

The operation had been very carefully planned; it was truly "top secret." The three soldiers chosen to carry out the operation were not informed of its objective until minutes before arriving at the palace in the VW. The arrest and removal of the sovereign had been demanded of the generals and colonels by an anonymous captain, the one who on June 28 had set up the headquarters of the Coordinating Committee for the Armed Forces, Police and Territorial Army in the 4th Military Division.

There is no official explanation of why such a small car was used. Unofficially, however, it has been rumored that there was no other car available; that they wanted to teach the Emperor a lesson; that they did not want to arouse the displeasure and possible anger of a people who, although involved in a mass, spontaneous uprising, were thought to have omitted Haile Selassie from the list of the guilty. Impelled by the most primitive fanaticism, with which they had been well inculcated, the people might well have attempted to liberate their everlasting political and religious chief, absolute dean of power in the world, the sovereign who had survived kings, presidents, Popes and patriarchs since the time of World War I.

Suddenly, however, the secret was out. As the car took the corner near the Djibouti railroad crossing at full speed, someone recognized the august person— the frail, shrunken body, all that was left of a dynasty that was three centuries old, a body wracked by the nausea of fear, yet still hoping for a miracle—and screeched at the top of his voice: "It's the Emperor! They've arrested him!" Everyone, including those who couldn't have had time to see him, saw him. Even more surprising, people on the streets along which the VW sped began to shout out loud something that the military chiefs hadn't even dared to whisper: "Thief! Murderer! Monster!" These were the same people who had gathered each afternoon on street corners where soldiers and policemen had been stationed, waiting for the big bullet-proof vehicle to make its customary stop, in the hope of delivering their naive petitions to the Emperor; the people whose supreme ambition had been to have their sons and daughters see the personage on the wide avenue in front of the Addis Ababa Hilton and be blessed by and receive some money from his sacred hands— sometimes after a traditional Sunday Coptic wedding; the people who once every 15 days had repaired to the palace to attend the Emperor's hearings—also attended by the nobles, for whom, of course, seats were provided in the great hall.

The Emperor's rulings in hearings on lawsuits between rich and poor, and between the poor themselves, were final. Hearings involving only the rich took place without too much of a crowd, in closed circles of elegant, perfumed courtiers, with their salaams and veiled smiles. But sometimes the hearings attracted many people, as when the Alfa Negus (literally "breath of the king") was invoked; this was the final appeal in cases which the Supreme Tribunal decided to leave to the sublime judgment of Ethiopia's pure giver of justice. Generally, the shouts of laughter coming from those seated in the hall drowned the tears of those standing, but no record was kept, and faith did not dwindle. The people continued to believe that the Emperor was good; the bad ones were his aides, his judges, his ministers—the evil spirits he would someday vanquish. How could it be otherwise, when Ethiopia was governed by a demigod whom the young people of the country believed to have no physiological needs? (I was told this by journalists on the *Ethiopian Herald*. There are grounds, then, for thinking that this was the reasoning not only of ignorant peasants but of children of the bourgeoisie with considerable educational background. When it occurred to one of them to doubt this (at about the age of 13) and he asked the teacher about it, he was told in no uncertain terms, "Of course he has no need to urinate. And, if he dies one day, the sun will stop shining. Who doesn't know that?")

Yet, as the VW sped away, feelings toward the Emperor had changed. "Thief! Murderer! Monster!" At some street corners, coins rained on the roof, windows and windshield of the car—fractions of *birs*, bearing the likeness of the Emperor, now a frightened bird, no longer able to fly so proudly on high and pluck out entrails. Black, bony hands, sometimes leprous hands, pulled coins out of goatskin bags, out of old tin cans, out of top hats recovered from the garbage can of some mansion or other, and hurled them at the vehicle. Had the car slowed down, it would have been stopped once and for all by the populace, and the Emperor would have perished at the hands of the beggars he had so wantonly created.

The arrest of a monarch who had been lord and master, judge and executioner, for the past 50 years snapped the last ideological shackles in the most spontaneous people's revolution in the history of Africa, and perhaps of the whole world. The Revolution had first broken out on February 13, 1974, set off by someone's protest in some Addis Ababa garage or gas station over the rise in the price of gas. It is said that it was a taxi driver who was so enraged that he got out of his car and set off down the street, shouting much as a street vendor would. Others soon joined him, their shouts generating a sudden and unexpected demonstration. Dozens, hundreds, thousands, marched through the streets chanting: "Down with the gas price rise!" When the crowd reached the entrance to the university, two opposing contingents swelled the ranks of the demonstrators: first the students and then the police, who had been stationed around the university and who found it difficult to break up what was by then a street riot by wielding their billy clubs and firing into the air. A second demonstration, staged by students, met with the same opposition. However, a third, held on the 16th, was permitted, and, according to eyewitnesses, nearly 100,000 people were involved in this one. So, on February 23, for the first time in half a century, the imperial government retreated, rescinding the price increase that had started the protests. By then, however, Addis Ababa had been turned upside down, and no way could be seen of restoring the peace. On the 18th, the teachers had gone on strike, uncharacteristically opposing the so-called Revision of the Educational Sector, a measure that went directly against their interests. On the 20th, the students and workers were out on the streets again with the first openly political demands of the incipient uprising, accusing the government of betraying the Emperor. This demonstration was hailed by the taxi drivers who, 48 hours earlier, had themselves gone on strike—a strike that was ended only after the government rolled back the increase in the price of gas. Horns honked gaily, and, amidst the shouting crowd, revolutionary songs of the international proletariat were heard for the first time in Ethiopia—mingled, of course, with the ritual cries of "Long live the Emperor!"

The Emperor sat in the back seat of the VW, which was driven by a soldier with a clean-shaven baby face that seemed solemn because of a diagonal scar. On the Emperor's left sat a second soldier; next to the driver was another. Haile Selassie clenched his teeth, held his breath—cold as the early morning air—not daring to think, as if all this were happening to somebody else, as if it were the moment in a nightmare to say: "It's only a dream." Only when the high iron gate at the end of the central avenue opened did he fully realize that this time the gate was not being opened just for him, because nobody saluted him. Perhaps no one knew who was in the car or . . . impossible! Even then his instinctive reaction was not a dramatic one. His thoughts centered on the fact that never before in his 80-odd years had he even considered traveling in such a small car. He remembered that he had made a gift of several such cars to his grandchildren a few weeks earlier and that even a 6-year-old great grandson had demanded, and received, one too—to the laughter of all, including the servants, althoughh had scolded the child somewhat. . . . These were his thoughts when he heard the shouts and the beating of coins on the roof and windows of the car. "My God, they've all gone mad!" Almost miraculously the small car with the little man inside made its getaway. The great revolution could now proceed peacefully, without violence or bloodshed, which was what its anonymous military leaders wanted.

The prisoner was confined to a large room in the garrison. Ten minutes later, a young officer entered the room and read him the document decreeing his removal. When the officer had finished, the former monarch asked for the name of the leader of the uprising.

"Mengistu? A relative of the man who tried to overthrow me in 1960? But no, he wouldn't have remained in the army. Anyway, when I return to the palace I will have to abolish that surname. . . ." He laughed until he heard the laughter of the officer who a minute before had read in a nervous whisper the decree issued by the Coordinating Committee.

They didn't read him the other edicts that meant the end of the decadent, immense power of Haile Selassie: repeal of the 1955 Constitution; dissolution of Parliament, until then openly based on the nobility, on feudal class lines; and abolition of the old foreign policy, that had been determined far away from Addis Ababa.

These three blows, all on the 12th, paved the way for setting up the Provisional Military Administrative Council (PMAC) three days later. This was to take the place of the Coordinating Committee and assume the functions of the head of state.

In this way, a certain duality of powers came to an end, and the military chiefs took command of the country. In effect, their assumption of power came about progressively rather than in a calculated manner, for it followed the spiral of the uprising of the masses in town and countryside.

ON FEBRUARY 23, by canceling the increase in the price of gasoline, the imperial government had thought it would put an end to the protest movement. However, the masses took this as a sign of weakness and continued their action; in addition, there was by now general alarm over the news of famine, after six years of continuous drought and official indifference. Demonstrations and strikes gave vent to the petitions of each and every sector of the country: from transportation workers to civil servants, from soldiers to firemen. It was as if everyone—except the Emperor—had something to demand, and urgently.

In the midst of this chaotic situation, Prime Minister Aklilou Habte-Wolde had had to hand in his resignation on February 27. He represented the decrepit feudal oligarchy, whose power had still seemed impregnable on February 12.

Revolutions will occur when the masses at the bottom can no longer tolerate to live in the old way and the rulers on top, in crisis, can no longer rule in the old way. This law, discovered by Marx and which guided Lenin in the October Revolution, was operating in Ethiopia.

Under these circumstances, on February 28, Endalkatchew Makonnen made his appearance on the scene as Ethiopia's new Prime Minister, sprouting high-sounding populist phrases. It was he who first declared that it was a time of change. Furthermore, as if heralding the setting up of an imperial government "as good as" the Emperor himself, a commission was appointed on March 25 to investigate scandals regarding the misuse of public funds and property, the sudden enrichment of state officials, and cases of obvious miscarriage of justice. Several members of the previous Cabinet were placed under house arrest, while the new Cabinet seemed to accept the judgment of Parliament (where no one had ever said anything against the government) that the former military officers who had been arrested for sympathizing with the first outbreak of popular protest, and for refusing to repress it, should be released.

Now, to the surprise of the skeptical military chiefs, on July 3 the new government agreed to work with the Coordinating Committee, just one week after the lat-

ter had been created. On July 4 it sanctioned the
execution of Dejazmatch Tsehayu, administrator of
Kaffa Province. His death, the first, occurred in the
Ensaro district of the Selale region, when he refused
to surrender to the members of the security forces.
His brother Fitaurari Tadesse and various accom-
plices were captured later. The imperial government
hailed the deed whose outcome the whole population
had awaited. On July 6, the Coordinating Committee
ordered former officers to return government property they had been illegally withholding, and at the
same time decreed the long-awaited amnesty of political prisoners. Finally, on the 8th, the famous watchword "Ethiopia Tikdem"—"Ethiopia First"—rang out
from the garrisons. Nationalist through and through,
the watchword reached thousands of exiles in many
countries, including sons of the ruling class who had
been in Paris during May 1968 and would soon fly
back home, their suitcases filled with Maoist book-
lets.

Rising in pitch, successive measures decreed the
abolition of two untouchable feudal institutions: the
Crown Council and the highest tribunal of justice, the
so-called Imperial Chilot Supreme Court.

In August, Jubilee Palace was renamed the National Palace. A few weeks earlier the government
had acceded to something that had long been desired
by the people in the economic field, when it froze rents
for houses and stores. To block the outflow of money,
the Minister of Finance became the only one to authorize withdrawal of funds.

The measures proposed by the Coordinating Committee clashed more and more with the uncom-
promising attitude of the Cabinet. Consequently, on
July 22 another Prime Minister was appointed. Lij
Mikael Imru thus came to hold the post, though this
did not mean any substantial change in government.

In an attempt to avert a blow from the rear, the office
of the Chief of Staff was transferred in mid-August

from the private quarters of the Emperor to the Ministry of National Defense. Immediately afterward, the
clean-up reached right under the imperial carpet: at
the peremptory request of the military, the National
Resources Development Share Company (an ideal
cover for the rich to get richer) became public property, and two days later—on August 27—the Ambassa
(Lion) Bus Company, which filled the coffers of the
aristocracy for 21 years, met the same fate. However,
it wasn't until September 5 that the dirt was found on
the supposedly spotlessly clean boots of the Emperor:
upon inspecting the books of the nationalized St.
George Brewery and the Haile Selassie Prize Trust, it
was discovered that the brewery had provided the
King of Kings with 11 million *birs* in dividends. The
people followed the news in the press; even the illiterate scanned the papers that soon sold out at the news-
stands and from newsboys' hands. The initial "He?
Impossible!" now gave way to doubt. The doubt increased when the mysterious accounts of the Charity
Trusts came to light. It was known that the Trust
consisted of five hospitals, three clinics, two orphanages, two homes for the aged and other similar
enterprises. Then it was revealed that it also owned
several hotels, other buildings and agricultural enterprises. Gradually, it became clear that the Emperor was a demigod obsessed with money. Finally, it
became known that his vast personal fortune might
well be one of the largest, if not the largest, in the
world. Soon it was also disclosed that he had deposited money in Switzerland.

On September 11, the Coordinating Committee invited the Emperor to bring that money home to help
solve the serious economic crisis the country was
going through. He was shown the figures compiled by
the Economic Committee for Africa and the UN Economic and Social Council. These figures revealed
that, since 1970, Ethiopia's Gross National Product
had grown only 1.6 percent annually. Since the per-

centage increase of the population had been 2.8, there had been a net loss of 1.2 per inhabitant in terms of the GNP. In agriculture alone, the figure was just about zero: 0.4, to be exact. In money terms, income per inhabitant was less than $90 a year.

The Coordinating Committee then appealed to the sentiments of the Emperor, who cared little about figures not related to his own bank accounts. It was already known by then that the fortune he had deposited in Switzerland amounted to billions of dollars.

On the evening of September 11, a heart-rending film that Haile Selassie's personal secret police believed to have been seized and destroyed was shown on TV. The Coordinating Committee had invited all the people to watch it and made the Emperor promise that he would watch it too—a promise that was kept. There were shouts of horror on the one side, and a few yawns on the other, as both watched the "premiere" of British journalist Jonathan Dimbleby's documentary, *The Hidden Hunger*.

The camera had been nosing around Wollo Province, sometimes so rapidly that the haste and fear of the cameraman were evident. The scenes filmed were reminiscent of Nazi concentration camps. Bones heaped high, skeletons of children mingled with those of the donkeys they drove carrying incredible loads, like the bicycles in Vietnam. The documentary also showed a parched land after years without rain, a land typical of Africa, the continent where it rains least and where relative evaporation is at its highest. Wasn't it true that the famine and the drought had been officially denied? Wasn't it true that, to prevent the spreading of rumors that would make the people in Addis Ababa uneasy, documentaries of the Emperor throwing huge pieces of juicy red meat to dogs and lions in the palace gardens had not been shown?

The Emperor was not moved by the scenes on TV; with regard to his money he merely pointed out that he had appointed his son heir to his fortune and that it was impossible for an Emperor to retract. "I'm really sorry," he said.

On September 12, at 7:30 A.M., Mengistu and his fellow officers carried out the legal overthrow of the diminutive big thief.

III

The Ethiopian Revolution, bent on preventing bloodshed at all costs, didn't even spill that of the one most to blame for the mountains of bleached bones along the dusty roads, the bones of at least 200,000 people.

The worst punishment for the Emperor, Mengistu argued before the Coordinating Committee, would be to place Ethiopia in the hands of those whose efforts for centuries had built it without its ever belonging to them.

It wasn't easy, however, to make the people their own master.

Haile Selassie lost all his titles but he left behind him an incredible record of iniquities and eccentricities: his tricornered hat a la Trujillo; his habit of ordering his ministers to come before him every morning—not to see him, for they had to approach him bowing with heads bent, but so that he might see them before they sat at their posts compelling others to suffer the very humiliation they had just suffered at his hands; his after-breakfast order to the four buglers he called into the dining room to sound their bugles from the corners of the palace roof and announce to all the kings of the world that their King now gave them leave to have breakfast; and other similar eccentricities, such as the one the author himself witnessed when Haile Selassie arrived in Cambodia for an official visit in 1969. After being greeted by Prince Sihanouk, when the band began to play the Ethiopian anthem the Emperor made a gesture for it to stop until Lulu, the royal dog, had descended from his personal Boeing jet. The Cambodian chief of state later confessed to some ambassadors, that he had been tempted to ask, "Your Majesty, may we start, or must we wait until the little dog has relieved herself?"

Naturally, when Lulu died, the Emperor shed the tears he had never shed for the 200,000 victims of famine in Wollo Province. Imperial funeral rites accompanied Lulu to her final resting place under a tombstone bearing her legendary name and dates of birth and death inscribed in gold. It must be admitted that the people also cried, with just as much sincerity. They cried with their Emperor, sharing his sorrow. The moment was photographed and filmed, and tales were told of it from mouth to mouth.

Gold, like that on Lulu's tomb, is also one of the wonders adorning the 200 palace chambers; it comes from the mines the Emperor secretly owned in Sidamo Province. Work at the mines was done by slaves, recruited by force, hunted down as in former times, when slave traders hunted Blacks in Africa for the European colonies of the Americas. . . . A construction worker, returning to his hut made of bare boards and a tin roof after 12 hours of toil for a wage scarcely double what some fortunate beggar might make—or one of the unemployed, roaming the streets at dawn, afraid that the police might beat him up, huddled in old newspapers to protect himself against the cold—might well be grabbed suddenly and thrown into a closed truck without windows. He wouldn't see the light of day again until he arrived at the mines. There he would spend the whole day bent over a creek, stopping only to eat his prison rations. Then, at night, believe it or not, he would be compelled to take a purgative, just in case some gold nuggets had gotten into his mouth while he was sifting sand. Special gendarmes then poked around in the feces, and if something glittered there, the culprit was sentenced without appeal.

The most striking thing is that the people as a whole were not aware that hundreds of men were kidnapped every year, and not one of those who did know suspected that the Emperor could possibly know about it, much less be the one responsible.

In his palace, with its 800 servants, the rugs on which he stepped every morning at around 11:00 o'clock were embroidered with gold. His toilet seat was solid gold, as were the bicycle frame for his daily exercises, the washstand and the bathtub. His clothes were something else; it depended on who was going to see them. There wasn't much gold on his clothes for evening outings, but those he wore when receiving ambassadors, or at official receptions, or on trips to other countries had as much gold as possible, with no limits dictated by even the most elementary good taste.

The Emperor had an insatiable appetite for gold, and it didn't let him rest. I have been told by intellectuals who were in frequent contact with him as interpreters for visits of foreign rulers (whose consciences are clear with regard to crime and abuse) that Haile Selassie was also obsessed by two fears: old age and death. On this score, he didn't turn to intellectuals educated in Rome or Paris.

"For such things, in Africa—our own ways."

He was referring to Ton Kuai, the witch doctor. Before Ton Kuai all his repressed pride, his believing himself to be the Elected of God, dissolved like the autumn mist that envelops Addis Ababa. On his knees, utterly sincere in his humility, bowed before his spiritual master, the physical master of all the people offered his pagan prayer and begged for strength and life.

A unique Cuban woman lives in Addis Ababa, at Kebele 08-0312, number 845. Rogelia Emiliana Leon (ID number 12) had a Congolese grandfather and is now an Ethiopian citizen. She was born and brought up in Guanabacoa but emigrated to Ethiopia in 1952 after marrying a young Ethiopian who had been taken to Cuba to study there, by a Cuban veterinarian named Barreras. Nobody quite knows when or how Barreras began to work on the Emperor's stud farm. The young man's father had foreseen the war of 1935 (when Mussolini attacked Ethiopia) and had persuaded his friend Barreras to take his son back to Cuba with him and have him trained as a rural teacher.

The wedding (they are now divorced) took place in Guanabacoa. In Addis Ababa, Rogelia learned Amharic and became Ethiopian by dint of destiny, but she didn't forget the socialist ideas her parents had taught her when she was a little girl. She told me a story that seems to have come out of a film like *The Exorcist*:

> I remember as if it were today, the day the principal of the school where I worked as a cleaning woman brought in 12 little Black girls, blacker than I, blacker than all the Ethiopians I have known in 25 years. They were so black you could hardly see their hair. This race lives on the Sudan border. It is a strong race. The girls were strong, too, and beautiful. Their ears hadn't been pierced, because they were Muslims, not Christians. When I saw them arrive, I thought they had been sent to school to be educated, to learn Amharic, since they spoke a dialect. I imagined that they would someday become the mistresses of some figure at the Court—maybe of the Emperor himself, who knows? But one day the principal told me the truth. Every year in December two of them were taken to the palace for the Emperor's birthday. Not this palace, the one in Bishoust, some 60 kilometers from here. The Debre-Sait Palace. Those two would never come back. When they left the school, all perfumed, they looked so pretty in their white dresses! When they got to the palace they were sacrificed, and their blood was cast into the palace lake. Then, alone, the Emperor bathed naked in that

water and drank of it. Then he allowed the servants and other people who were around to
plunge into the lake. The girls were so naive
that, when they saw the portrait of the Emperor
with the "three Selassies"—what's it called? . . .
the Holy Trinity! . . . the Emperor was the fourth
saint or something like that—they bowed and
said "Father." This went on for five consecutive
years, each December. I don't know what they
told the ones who remained in the school; possibly they had the girls believe that the others had
returned to their hamlets. When there were only
two left, the principal couldn't stand it any longer, and she decided to save Debritu, the heavier
girl who was very intelligent, and the other,
whose name I've forgotten, who was even pret-
tier, and slim. In mid '73, or '72, she had their ears
pierced, as if they had been baptized. This way
they were of no use for the blood bath. And as far
as I know, no one said anything, because the
Coptic religion was so strong that even the
Crown respected it. . . . A year ago I found out
that Debritu had finished the twelfth grade and
the other, the ninth. . . . As for the blood bath,
well, the explanation was that the Devil lived in
the lake, and he wanted the Emperor to grow old
and frail. To appease him, they had to give him
Muslim blood, the blood of that pure, innocent
race. I don't know. . . . But I do know that the
Emperor came to the throne through murder.
The Queen was married to Yasu, a prince. Haile
Selassie wanted to be king. He poisoned the
prince at a dinner and married the widow. They
say she was already pregnant and that that explains why the Emperor despised his eldest son,
who wasn't his, and preferred Makonnen, his
second son, who died in an accident—though it's
also said that he was killed by a jealous pilot. I
worked also as a cleaning woman in the hospital
at night, to earn more money. They didn't let the
doctor or anybody see the corpse. I know many
stories like this. The Emperor was a terrible
man, a real monster.

2 A Revolution Seeking Its Ideology

I

THE 1974 Ethiopian Revolution has no precedent. There have been countless spontaneous uprisings, but the classes in revolt, though they groped instinctively for an ideology to explain their origins and actions, had not—right from the outset—embraced Marxism-Leninism.

Notwithstanding the reactionary political ideas of Hegel and Feuerbach, Marx saw in their philosophies the earliest roots of the ideology of the proletariat. Neither Hegel nor Feuerbach, in spite of their genius, would have been able to discover these roots—let alone develop them, thereby defying the social order they served. It was Marx and his alter ego, Engels, who were far more profound thinkers and of purer hearts, who were to become the teachers of the class destined by history to bury along with its chains all slavery, all humiliation and all fear. The fathers of the revolution predicted that the working class would overthrow bourgeois rule and, after the period of its own inevitable dictatorship, consolidate its victory and build a new society without exploiters, making the transition to a humanized mankind, with no classes, frontiers or state.

Lenin said and proved that the proletariat had to act in alliance with other exploited classes, first and foremost with the peasants.

Marx and Engels believed in a single world revolution. Lenin, having drawn attention to the uneven development of capitalism in different countries and areas, made it quite clear that the proletarian revolution could take place and triumph in certain places before others—in those where the contradictions were most sharply developed and where there were forces capable of resolving and eliminating those contradictions. The awareness that revolution was knocking at the door came from acting on the working-class ideology set down for the exploited and the oppressed by scientists who were not born in the working class.

The fusion of the working class with its class ideology takes place through the work of the Party. With the appearance of the Party, the working class begins to change from a "class in itself"—one that doesn't know what it wants and is blindly exploited—to a "class for itself," that already works for its total liberation. This process culminates in the taking of power.

Marx and Engels founded the first party of the proletariat in several countries at the same time: namely, the First International, a tremendous feat in itself. Even though the First International didn't guide the tactics of or even foster the 1871 Paris Commune—that incredible, surprising "assault on the heavens" which threw off the bourgeois yoke for the first time, though only for three months and in only one city—it was in the International that the heroic Communards learned the strategy of beginning social change by taking political power.

Lenin specifically created the new-style party as the general staff of and for the revolution. Afterward he led it to victory in the Great October Socialist Revolution, which gave birth to the first worker-peasant state in history, and affirmed that the time had come for workers to free themselves.

The Soviet Union—an infant barely out of the cradle—had to mature quickly and become strong, daring and wise, in order to assert its existence through blood, sweat and fire. It faced its supreme test against fascist aggression, the cruelest imperialist response to socialism.

The main result of that encounter was that socialism crossed the barrier of national frontiers: socialism became one of two world systems, now engaged in final struggle. For the first time in history, it looked as if there were a hope of imposing peace on earth. History records at least 14,000 important wars, including two world wars. With the establishment of the socialist camp (which declared the death sentence for the old colonial system and weakened the base of world imperialism), the possibility emerged of having a revolution without its being the product of war.

Ethiopia shows something else, as well: without the way being prepared openly by ideology, in Ethiopia the people first made their Revolution—using the means created to prevent it (that is, the old army)— and then their Revolution began to discover itself and its ideology.

This doesn't mean that the ideological factor can be dispensed with in making the revolution. On the contrary. It means that, today, Marxist-Leninist ideology penetrates so deeply everywhere, in all circles throughout the world with such strength, that it reaches even those places where books are burned and popular parties are considered to be as criminal as the reading of revolutionary works. It is like breathing unconsciously through one's pores after having been ordered to cover one's nose and mouth.

As Fidel indicated during his visit to Ethiopia, its Revolution proves the truth that class struggle rules history.

We shouldn't express wonder at this advance of Marxism-Leninism in a country where there were no Marxist-Leninists anywhere. There were workers; there were the peasant masses; there was a people exploited to the hilt, beaten, crushed, offended and tricked; and even though the people had been deceived for decades into accepting their fate and adoring the leader of their class enemies as if he were a god, one day the water overflowed and became the torrent that is the revolution, as Julio Antonio Mella put it.

The Ethiopian Revolution has been spontaneous in the sense that nobody determined in advance the date on which it was to break out; therefore, there were no advance preparations in terms of organization and education.

When, all of a sudden, conditions are ripe for revolution, it is obvious that the revolution stands on much firmer ground when a vanguard force of workers and peasants is organized and educated to recognize the *right moment*—the one that, as Lenin said, can be neither a minute too early, for then it would be premature, nor a minute too late, because the opportunity might be lost—for the mass of workers and peasants to take the offensive.

Ethiopia confirms completely that the 20th century can be the last to have societies divided into antagonistic classes. The exploited, the oppressed, those who have nothing to lose but their chains, can defeat their enemies.

The spontaneous nature of the Ethiopian Revolution confirms the fact that the moment for change has arrived. Even where no storm is forecast, where trouble clouds seem very distant, a hurricane may develop from a single flash of lightning or from some first invisible whirlwind and sweep everything away. The 2,000-year-old empire vanished in three days.

One by one, the myths that paralyze the masses or prevent them from achieving total victory die.

With the triumph in 1959, of the Cuban Revolution, led by Fidel Castro, not only did socialism reach the Americas, but a double myth based on geography was shattered; it held that no revolutionary sun could last in the shadow of the United States and that no socialist state could be created far from immediate geographical contact with the USSR. With their revolutions directed against the US armed forces, Vietnam,

Laos and Cambodia have finished off such lies for good and all.

Next, the people of Angola, like the people of Mozambique before them, were victorious in their struggle against NATO-buttressed Portuguese colonialism and backed the MPLA when Agostinho Neto proclaimed true independence. Then the people had to prepare to withstand invasion by imperialism's big gendarme in Africa, the racist-fascist Pretoria regime, and its small gendarme and clown, Mobutu, Haile Selassie's emulator and Zaire's satrap—both entrenched behind forces encouraged and armed by the Peking regime, itself a traitor to socialism.

Cuba gave internationalist support to the Angolan resistance, and here, as in Vietnam, Soviet solidarity confronted the imperialist resources that were thrown on the side of oppression.

Ethiopia follows the same process but in a qualitatively new way.

Vietnam had a Leninist Party forged by Ho Chi Minh to guide the various stages of the resistance against colonialism and neocolonialism and turn it into a socialist revolution.

In Cuba, in the midst of a century of struggle, first against Spanish colonialism and then against Yankee neocolonialism, a party of the proletariat was born after Lenin's October Revolution which was to march forward to meet the movement that was to give birth to the Revolution on July 26, 1953, with the attack on the Moncada Garrison. From this battle emerged the leader of the Revolution and the tactical program that brought together and mobilized all the people on the one path on which they could be educated collectively.

In the incomparable school of their own revolutionary experience, the Cuban people adopted the Marxist-Leninist ideas that Fidel had searched for and held since his student days. Two of those ideas guided him more than any others: those of relying on the masses and of winning true revolutionary power with and for them.

That party, the movement and the anti-imperialist student organization that had been created to fight the dictatorship were fused to form the Communist Party of Cuba, which constitutes the heart and mind of the present process of building socialism. Seniority within the Party is rightly counted from the time of the invasion at Playa Giron, the Bay of Pigs, in 1961, an open confrontation between revolutionary Cuba and counterrevolutionary imperialism.

In Angola, the liberation struggle was headed by a movement, the MPLA, which is being turned into a party of the working class and socialism. Something similar is happening in Mozambique with FRELIMO, founded by Eduardo Mondlane, the leadership of which was taken up by Samora Machel after Mondlane's death.

In Ethiopia, however, there was neither a classical Marxist-Leninist Party nor a civilian revolutionary movement. There wasn't even any secret military group, such as Nasser's Free Officers in Egypt or, later, el-Qaddafi's in Libya—which were connected with the Muslim religion and tended to reach toward the people.

The head of the Ethiopian Revolution, Lieutenant Colonel Mengistu Haile Mariam, has said that, due to the fact that the Revolution broke out spontaneously, at a time when there was no working-class party ("the firmest guarantee of the Revolution"), it wasn't possible to avoid many of the bitter struggles now rampant.

How could a revolution possibly triumph without a party? How could there be a revolution without some organized revolutionary movement?

The answers to these questions provide a truly great lesson in dialectics. The objective conditions of poverty and oppression pushed the popular masses into action with growing determination, which increased at the same rate as the imperial government maneuvered and drew back. The process of gestation didn't even take nine months: after eight, Haile Selassie was dethroned and the Revolution triumphed once and for all.

The initial character of the popular uprising was the usual one of a national democratic revolution; as such, it was antifeudal, anti-imperialist and opposed to the bureaucratic bourgeoisie. The soldiers joined it en masse. But the right-wing officers in the army had been conspiring since February 13, 1974, to hold back the revolution. At first they tried to limit the revolution to simple reform; later, they resorted to outright counterrevolution.

The right wing began by trying to reduce the change to a simple attempt to modernize the old state organization, which had broken down through anachronism and corruption. As a general who did not wish to identify himself ironically declared in March 1974, to a correspondent of a foreign capitalist news agency, the old state had fallen apart "at the shouts of a few taxi drivers, students and workers."

Apart from its mass, spontaneous nature—which could only be upheld on the basis of a class struggle which, though not recognized as such by the classes engaged in it, existed and increased until it reached the boiling point—the most surprising thing about the Ethiopian Revolution was that the leadership was taken by the armed forces. Such a surprise had a hidden logic: it had to be the army or no one. If not, Ethiopia would have become a society without any social order at all.

The objective situation of a country lacking a true government when it most needed it, with the mass of the people having no ideological or organizational vehicle that could implant a new social order, gave the army—the only institution still on its feet amidst the uprising, economic disaster, famine and confusion—a sort of mandate to rule.

But to rule in whose name? At the service of which class? In alliance with which of the two large international forces operating in the world?

It is evident today that, although it is true that Marxism-Leninism in Ethiopia hadn't penetrated strongly enough to create a party or a movement, the universality of socialist ideas had indeed reached the middle officer class. One of them, the son of a slave, had experienced racial discrimination in the United States, even though he had been there as a cadet of a monarch pampered by Washington. He had also known about the war in Vietnam, the Detroit fires started by the Black masses, the student rebellion and the general unease that, later on, led to the Watergate scandal. Through his experience in the United States, Mengistu began to get a clear view of the present world with its irrepressible increase of revolutions, rebellions and conflicts.

Upon his return, that young captain encountered the abyss between imperial luxury and the hunger of the masses of his country.

The language in which *The Communist Manifesto* was written became the essence of truth to him. Without any hesitation, he sided with the exploited, the oppressed and the humiliated in Ethiopia, and when he saw them spontaneously taking to the streets in raging protest in Asmara and Addis Ababa, he felt himself one with them. What is more, he decided to promote a movement for making demands within the armed forces and, above all, to promote the revolutionary idea that soldiers should not fire on the people. This gave a particular stamp to the Coordinating Committee of the Armed Forces which the army chiefs didn't dare to oppose, for they realized that hanging on to the Emperor and his dying regime was tantamount to holding on to a sinking ship on the high seas in the midst of a storm. These chiefs, not without the advice of some of their 300 US military advisers, willingly became members of the Coordinating Committee.

At the same time, perhaps through fear of violating the hierarchy, which would have wreaked havoc with the only institution that had managed to escape social anarchy, Lieutenant General Aman Mickael Andom, chief of the armed forces, was named President of the Coordinating Committee.

Despite this, the Revolution was still weak, since the man appointed to be the leader of the Revolution, though indeed a leader, was not a revolutionary.

The Ethiopian Spínola did everything within his power to control the spontaneous process that had raised him to his post. He hid his sword in demagogical words, holding it ready to strike treacherously from within.

His recent crimes, together with many others that had helped him to attain his position under someone like Haile Selassie, finally led him, together with 60 other high-ranking officers, to the firing squad. That was on November 24, 1974.

The military roster then gave the leadership of the PMAC to Brigadier General Teferi Bente, with Mengistu as First Vice President and Lieutenant Colonel Atnafu Abate as Second Vice-President.

The struggle for power continued, since Bente was a hidden but determined enemy of the ideology being adopted by the Revolution. Led by that enmity, rooted in the prejudices and ambitions of the exploiting class, he took up the threads of the conspiracy of Andom to weave with them the shroud for the revolutionary process he had joined at the last minute.

Three years minus ten days after the outbreak of the Revolution, Mengistu took over the leadership, and it was then that the Revolution finally took the route that was to lead it to final and lasting victory.

What is this Revolution, and what does it consist of?

To answer this question, the first step would be to analyze Ethiopia's history, economy, society and politics, and this would have to be done by analyzing the man who believed himself a demigod and whose dethronement resulted in the Revolution.

3 When Haile Selassie Fought for Power

I

IN 1916 a palace coup d'etat in Addis Ababa dethroned a child emperor.

Emperor Lij Yasu, grandson of Menelik II, the founder of the Ethiopian state, was dethroned—although, actually, he was so young that he hardly wielded any power. The coup was really directed against the regent, Ras Taffari, an ambitious young man.

In the absence of a male in the line of succession, Zauditu, the daughter of Menelik II, then came to the imperial throne.

The regent, who was the son of Ras Makonnen, a victorious general in the Italian-Ethiopian war of 1895-96, did not accept this loss of the power he had held until then, and, in effect, maintained a second organ of rule.

This duality of power reflected the acute contradiction that was developing within the ruling classes rather than a clash of personal ambitions.

On the one hand, the most conservative circles of the feudal nobility rallied around the Empress. They were the large landowners and the high clergy, who favored formal rather than effective state unity, thus presenting the country to the world as a single country, while actually it was divided into numerous regions, each under a small emperor, or *ras* (governor, military chief). The Coptic churches and monasteries owned large plots of land and feared centralization.

On the other hand were the commercial petty bourgeoisie and the few intellectuals who had emerged in Ethiopia. Their motto was "One Ethiopia," implying a strong central government. Their movement was called the Ethiopian Youth, and their leader was Ras Taffari Makonnen—he, who, driven by a lust for power, had become regent.

A third faction, somewhat neutral, was the army.

This political struggle was waged against the background of a most contradictory society, in which slavery was interlaced with a primary form of feudalism and tribal holdovers. To make this already crowded picture complete, a voracious incipient capitalism had been tacked on.

Although deep-rooted and ruthless, the political struggle being waged on high was not everything; nor was it the essential thing. A fundamental class struggle was developing in a spontaneous and sometimes violent form between the peasants and the cruel, allpowerful feudal masters who exploited them. For a long time, the communal peasant land had been diminishing; indeed, only a few isolated patches in faraway regions were left. Each peasant had to work from 90 to 120 days a year for the owner (the feudal lord or the church) of the poor plot of land allotted him. The peasant also had to give payment in kind (either a part of the crop or some cattle, depending on the type of economy), perform certain duties and comply with certain whims. To this exploitation and oppression were added state taxes and any other taxes the landowner chose to levy.

Two kinds of crown taxes were particularly severe: the *dergo* and the *gabar*.

The first placed the peasant under an obligation to feed and serve all nobles, officers and public officials who might be traveling through or camping out in his region. It sufficed for them to say they had an order to this effect from the *ras*.

The *gabar* supported the military and state appara-

tus even more directly. Peasant families had to guarantee the upkeep of local garrisons and administrations. The *gabar* levied increased with the recipient's
rank. Thousands of peasants were obliged to pay
gabar dues to governors and other high-ranking per-
sonages. Each family had to support at least one
soldier as well as surrender its sons to the army.

However, oppressed as they were, the peasants
were not the worst off in Ethiopian society. The slaves
who worked in feudal homes and, to a lesser extent, in
the fields had an even worse life. It must be noted,
however, that their number in the '30s was not as high
as the Mussolini press made out in its attempt to
justify Italy's fascist attack.

The three court movements all agreed on maintaining feudalism, but the Ethiopian Youth, trying to
piece things together and centralize the state, favored
development of the productive forces and a certain
degree of modern civilization. This group advocated a
growing home market, elimination of slavery and of
the subsistence production practiced in conservative
sectors, and the introduction of a money economy. In
this sense, they moved with history; this movement
was, relatively speaking, the most advanced.

At one point, this movement concentrated its efforts
on demanding the abolition of slavery, knowing that
the Empress would stubbornly oppose it even though
the decline of slavery was inevitable. Already, by the
middle of the 19th century, Theodore II had abolished
the slave trade; toward the end of the century, Menelik
II decreed that only prisoners of war could be made
slaves, and later he limited slavery to a period of
seven years. In 1924 another decree defined the cate-
gories of slaves to be freed and established how and
when this was to be done. This decree also stated that
slaves serving in the army were to be freed immediately.

In practice, such conditions lent themselves to the
"later or never" syndrome and tended to suppress

overt slavery, letting covert slavery exist; nonetheless, the conservative and the clergy deemed them revolutionary. The Empress used to say, "If something changes in some respect, everything might change in every respect."

In 1926, when the undeclared struggle between the regent, Ras Taffari Makonnen, and the Empress regarding slavery and how to abolish it was nearing the breaking point, the Minister of War died; this favored the regent by allowing him to take control of the army. As a result, he was able to quell two rebellions which the Empress openly encouraged against him two years later. In 1930, after the failure of a third attempt, headed by her former husband, the Empress died. Even though she had not held any real power for a long time, her funeral was magnificent. And Ethiopia had a new Emperor in its long and tortuous 3,000-year history. The regent appointed himself Emperor, with the name of Haile Selassie I. On at last coming to the throne he had coveted, little did he imagine that he was destined to be the last of the Ethiopian emperors.

II

The new monarch energetically set about completing the expansion of feudalism, but within very precise boundaries, now established from Addis Ababa.

This process had begun during the previous century, toward the end of which international imperialism, scarcely out of its cradle, had proceeded to the Repartition of Africa at the famous Berlin Conference of 1895. Europe was hungry for raw materials, markets, spheres of influence and cheap labor. The efforts at centralization in Ethiopia served also as a barrier to European expansion.

What was the picture under these circumstances?

The feudal aristocracy in Ethiopia conquered its opponents in the north and was ready to fall upon the south in order to have the whole country ruled by one state. Haile Selassie speeded up the achievement of his purpose in order to counter the imminent repartition of the country by European governments. Consequently, he needed the people's backing—though, for class reasons, he didn't look for popular support through any form of democracy but rather inculcated absolute submission, complete fanaticism and total imperial control. "I am Ethiopia," was the way his mind ran, and he tried to make all Ethiopians think the same way.

Julio Antonio Mella referred to the Cuban dictator Machado as a tropical Mussolini. Haile Selassie was a feudal Mussolini, aspiring to be a demigod.

In order to become the undisputed political chief, Haile Selassie first became regent and then military chief. Once he had a firm political grip, he tried to ensure himself lasting power by making himself the spiritual leader of the people.

The Coptic Church in Ethiopia had split off from the Roman Catholic Church in the 5th century but, once freed from the Vatican, had fallen under the patronage of Egypt. All but one of its bishops were Egyptians and were appointed by the Patriarch of Alexandria. Since England controlled Egypt at that time, the British had an excellent indirect way of interfering in the internal affairs of Ethiopia.

It was only in 1929 that Addis Ababa reached an agreement with Cairo whereby the rules of the game were changed: in the future, the Patriarch would only appoint the *Abuna* (Archbishop), whereas the Ethiopian bishops would be chosen from among the local clergy. Some 20 years later (in 1951), Ethiopia succeeded in appointing the *Abuna* as well. All this created an ideal climate for imbuing the personality cult of the Emperor with a certain aura of mysticism. His portrait was hung in the churches. Prayers in his honor preceded sermons. Even phrases and actions attributed to Christ were held to be those of Haile

Selassie. Well-known German artists painted scenes depicting Christ with the poor, giving Christ the Emperor's face, and these paintings were hung in full view. Even on altars, the Holy Trinity was supplemented by the kind, well-shaven face with half-closed eyes of the man who had added the title of God's Elected to that of Emperor. In addition, official propaganda, in an effort to please all, compared him with David, King of the Hebrews.

Haile Selassie purported to be a descendant of the Queen of Sheba and King Solomon. Right from the cradle, Ethiopian children were told the legend of how they met: how, at the beginning, the Queen, being very chaste, refused to marry the King; and how he, a sage among sages, made a wager with her that if she got up in the night to drink some water, they would be married. Of course, Solomon fixed it so her thirst would be stronger than her iron will to remain a virgin.

Finally, claiming the antiquity of the Ethiopian monarchy—the oldest on earth—and the victory of Emperor Theodore over Islam in 1855, the royal official title came to include that of King of Kings, which undoubtedly made many a European monarch smile, though none of them dared quarrel with the Emperor over such a trifling vanity, quite unimportant when compared to Ethiopia's riches and geographical position.

III

In social terms, Ethiopia experienced no substantial changes during the half century of Haile Selassie's autocratic rule.

His work as a ruler consisted essentially in carrying through the process of consolidating the power of the feudal aristocracy which had started at the beginning of the 19th century. In order to achieve this, it was necessary to win over other, less intel ligent sectors of the aristocracy that were more firmly attached to frankly anachronistic forms of production and ways of thinking. Haile Selassie was a sort of Bismarck, but without abandoning the class positions of feudalism. He became as little bourgeois as possible. He feared, and rightly so, that capitalist economic development would lead to the development of the working class, open the country to revolutionary ideas, and further the growth of the intelligentsia, who would first wonder at but later find repugnant his deification and greed for riches, power and personal glory.

At the same time, Haile Selassie's firm opposition to the European colonial powers' dismembering the country was to contribute to his being accorded maximum authority by the nation. The egotism characteristic of his class, his self-idolatry and his tyrant's greed were to lead him to abuse that authority.

Haile Selassie was a true representative of the feudal lords who, since 1880 (and even before), had opposed European incursions into the southern, southwestern and eastern parts of the country, thus preventing its falling under foreign control, and who had also been gradually centralizing state power through a complex process subsequently completed by Haile Selassie himself. As such, there is a logical thread to his policy, accounting for the stand he took in the face of fascism and for his international reputation.

Internally, the system was feudal through and through; it couldn't be anything but that, and there was never any intention of its being otherwise. As feudal rule advanced from the north toward the center and south of that enormous country, measuring more than a million square kilometers (the tenth largest country in the African continent), the condition of the peasants became worse and worse. The peasant community saw itself sentenced to death, despite the paternalism of the weaker lords.

The peasant masses became serfs—slaves, in fact. Haile Selassie abolished the enslavement of prisoners of war, only to have the mass of the working people toil under slave conditions.

In fact, in 1931, an imperial decree appeared granting immediate freedom to slaves at the funeral of their master. Four years later, slavery as such was declared abolished. In compliance with this decree, 1,427 slaves were freed in 1933, and 3,647 the following year, according to official figures. Nevertheless, there were many who died as slaves long after 1935. The government did not enforce the abolitionist laws with any great zeal, and the lords, the church, the merchants, high-ranking officers and public officials did everything they could to let the chains rust in place.

The reformation of feudal institutions was an even slower process than the abolition of slavery and was always handled so as to retain the essentials of feudalism: the idea was simply to give it attributes more in accord with the triumph of the bourgeoisie in the world as a whole.

It was only in May 1935 that the Ethiopian Youth, then in power, decided to pass a law eliminating the *gabar* system, which had been promised from the time they were in the opposition 20 years before. Only in one province did this new law become effective, and there only because the constant angry activities of the peasants threatened to develop into uprisings. The *dergo,* too, was suppressed more in theory than in practice.

Reforms in the political sphere were somewhat more effective. These were favorable to the ruling feudal class, because they made order much more ... orderly. The reforms didn't benefit the people in any way.

The first Constitution of the Ethiopian State (1931) made its centralization binding. The capital was Addis Ababa—which, in turn, centered around the

Emperor. A Parliament with two houses was cleverly designed so as not to overshadow the absolute monarch: he alone could appoint the senators. The members of the lower house were elected by and from among the noblemen, but always subject to prior consultation with the Emperor. In any case, the powers of this ornamental Parliament were limited to approving imperial decrees.

Like any modern state, Ethiopia required a professional army. After searching for a foreign power that wouldn't covet Ethiopia, the Emperor asked Belgium for military advice. The first pilots were trained by Belgium while the first airport was being built and the first military planes were being purchased in Brussels.

After 12 years in power, Haile Selassie had no reason to be proud of his work in the field of education. Nevertheless, he was. The 30 elementary and secondary schools that existed in 1930 appeared to him to be a lot. When he was overthrown in 1974, after ruling for half a century, 95 percent of the population could neither read nor write, and there were only about 6,000 university students in a country of 30 million inhabitants.

On the other hand, the capital was conveniently remodeled. The cold heights of Mount Entotto, (altitude over 8,000 feet), with a river and an extraordinary beautiful, lush landscape, were just the right setting for erecting a shell of luxury: wide avenues and palaces, where the surrounding slums wouldn't be noticed by guests at the centrally located modern hotels, such as the splended Hilton.

In 1887 the capital had been named Addis Ababa ("new flower" in Amharic). It was claimed that it was the resurgence of Ababa, the capital established several centuries before in another part of the country. Menelik II, who established the title of Emperor, was also the founder of a single capital for the whole country.

Some archaeological discoveries came to the support of the sick self-idolatry of Haile Selassie. One of the theories on the birth of mankind maintains that this could have taken place in or around Ethiopia. A village was unearthed in Gambore which was thought to be about one and a half million years old; fossils, tools and other objects were found, including the skeleton of a young woman about 20 years old who was thought to have lived about 4 million years ago.

The country has its own official language: Amharic, whose alphabet is of hieroglyphic origin, dating from the time of the Queen of Sheba. This language, as well as those of other countries in the region, goes back to the 4th century B.C. It is a Semitic language derived from Geez, the language of the Coptic Church, whose scripture it uses, but to which vowels were added to enable it to be spoken by the illiterate masses. The second language is Afan Oromo, or Galla, which 16th century migrations spread through Ethiopia. Since the Gallas are more numerous than the Amharas, their language is the one most widely spoken; the Amharas, however, have always been the dominant group. Actually, there are dozens of languages and dialects spoken among the 80-odd nationalities in Ethiopia.

Haile Selassie not only didn't solve the national problem; he made it worse. As a representative of the most powerful group, of Amharic origin, he always tried to discriminate against and oppress the other nationalities. This was more than just a struggle of interest: it was an attempt to take attention off the only true division—that between the classes.

The Revolution would inherit the national problem, primarily that of Eritrea and Ogaden. Imperialism, Arab reactionaries and internal counterrevolutionary class forces viewed this problem as the Achilles' heel of the only historical process that could solve it: the revolutionary, socialist process.

Haile Selassie found and left a country which was

predominantly agricultural. What little industrial development there was in Ethiopia (it should be remembered that this contradicted the myth of a demigod with no material interests) had taken place for the personal advantage of the Emperor. As a king of feudal lords, he was practically the only bourgeois in the ruling class.

In 1974 industry contributed only 8 percent or less of the Gross National Product. Agriculture accounted for over 90 percent. But, paradoxically, only a fifth of the arable land was being tilled. One of the reasons for this was social: feudalism. The other was climatic: the higher lands were preferred. The rural population has been concentrated from time immemorial in the northern and central regions. The density of the population there is far greater than in the south.

Haile Selassie found and left a large mass of landless peasants (at least 2.4 million out of a total 6 million); these peasants had had to settle under feudal conditions on the lands of absentee owners. They handed over 50 to 75 percent of their agricultural produce in rent. When the great drought in Wollo Province killed 1 percent of the population, the survivors realized that the blame lay with the typically feudal system of land tenure, which didn't allow the peasants to build up stores for such eventualities, and that it was this that kept them undernourished, halfnaked, working 14 hours a day with wooden hoes used centuries ago. This was another blow dealt the sinking empire, one that made the man who personified it hated even more.

The misery, poverty and helplessness of the masses was in sharp contrast to the opulence, waste and luxury at the other end of the scale.

A single family of landowners, the Biry family, in Harer Province, owned about 20 million hectares of land and ruled over the lives of 700,000 peasants.

Was it strange, then, that in 1976 the head of that family fell in combat while leading what amounted to a private army, after having burned, killed and engaged in all kinds of sabotage, in opposition to an agrarian reform that didn't acknowledge his late father's title of *ras* and that made the peasants who had been his father's serfs their own masters? Was it then, surprising that the peasants hunted him day and night until they captured him, as if he were one of the wolves that haunt the outskirts of Addis Ababa?

Naturally, back in the time of the fascist aggression, the Emperor in exile had had to make promises to the people in order to strengthen their heroic resistance—in which they never gave the enemy any respite and put an end to the fascist occupation four years before the fall of fascism as such.

After the victory over the Italian invader, the masses demanded that the promises be kept; in their political naiveté, they believed that the Emperor was their best friend. They saw him not as a part of the system but above it: a good master to all, somewhere between heaven and earth, between God and man.

In 1942 new decrees were issued, ratifying the abolition of slavery. In 1950 there were no slaves to be seen, but those who had once been chained simply became poor peasants and servants subjected to all kinds of humiliation.

At last the *gabar* system was buried along with slavery. In the future, money from the national budget would be set aside for keeping up the local military establishments, and officers would receive set salaries from Addis Ababa rather than commandeering the scanty food of peasant families. But eternal poverty remained, and the peasants continued to supply funds for the public treasury. Ethiopia was still the old Ethiopia, though it was becoming modernized.

The tax system was also changed somewhat. A money tax was levied not only on cultivated land but also on land that was lying idle. This led to the growth of a rural bourgeoisie. In some cases, merchants and bureaucrats from the cities puchased idle land. In other cases, the landowners increased the amount of their land that was planted to crops. Occasionally they returned to the state land which they had taken.

Haile Selassie was the state, so he could be generous in distributing large plots of land among the incipient rural bourgeoisie, largely made up of his friends from the Ethiopian Youth and in the administration. Since the Emperor encouraged the large landowners to become bourgeois, showing them that it was easier to get agricultural wage laborers than peasants and that they could obtain higher dividends, the changes were accepted without too much protest.

The official propaganda that flooded Africa presented Haile Selassie as a father of agrarian reform. The church constituted the biggest obstacle. The clergy opposed all change until the Emperor bribed and thus controlled it. The position of the church was that feudalism should go on exactly as before.

Thus, capitalism made *some* inroads in Ethiopia—without, however, doing away with the two basic classes in its history: the exploiting feudal lords and the exploited peasants. Haile Selassie managed to set himself up as supreme arbiter, above the struggles for power and conflicting interests. All turned to him.

In 1950, tired of waiting for the Emperor to learn about their misery—he complained it was the courtiers who didn't tell him the truth—the peasant masses in Gojam Province openly rebelled against their feudal masters. They could hardly believe it when the troops of the imperial army were ordered to fight on the side of the landowners and against them. The same thing happened in the south, at the end of the '50s. Hundreds of peasants died crying "Long live the Emperor!"

While mercilessly crushing revolts, Haile Selassie perfected the art of shedding tears over the abuses of good children who paid no attention to his advice or to Christian rules. He counseled the feudal lords to be moderate and even set up a Special Committee to administer justice on the agrarian question, which had become uppermost on the agenda.

The relief measures—only skin-deep—included the distribution of state-owned plots of land among the hungriest peasants and the granting of loans. In 1961 some of the state land in Arussi Province, near the capital, was distributed among the men who worked it, and they were offered loans with which to purchase it.

Continuing with his theatrical performances, in 1965 the Emperor put his signature to a law establishing a maximum of 50 percent of the crops to be paid as rent in kind, and then only if the peasant used draft animals and seeds supplied by the landowner. The law also forbade the feudal lord from drawing upon the pockets of "his" peasants in order to pay his own taxes. After this law was signed, peasants throughout the country and students in Addis Ababa acclaimed the Emperor. The House of Representatives soon passed the law, but the Senate vetoed it. The Emperor promised that he would go on fighting for his peasant people.

In 1955 a new Constitution had been introduced which differed from the former one in form only. The language was more refined and demagogic, and it certainly contained promises—later to be embodied in supplementary laws—as to certain social changes. Of course, the essence of the system remained unchanged. Imperial power was becoming even more entrenched. Thus, the lower house was to be elected by universal, secret ballot, to render it more sensitive to popular pressure. The Senate would still be appointed by the forefinger wearing the most dazzling jewels in the world.

Nevertheless, the 1957 electoral campaign provided an opportunity—albeit very small—for public debate, an innovation of great importance in a country which had never had any at all. On various platforms and in newspapers, the agrarian reform that was sup posedly sponsored by the Emperor was advocated. In December 1960, the revolt led by the officer named Mengistu broke out in Addis Ababa. It failed but it offered a novelty: its slogan was that of *imposing* reform, and it was the forerunner of the 1974 army revolt against the Emperor.

Haile Selassie then wanted to proceed on less dangerous grounds: education. You can't say that he did much, or even all that was possible, but he did do something. In 1950 he opened a university—for the sons and daughters of the rich, naturally. He gave it the name which he regarded as most honorable and magnificient—his own—and some good buildings. He also allowed young people to study abroad, especially in the United States.

In addition, he founded a library, a few theaters and some movie houses.

A figure was reached that seemed a record to him: 5 percent of the child population could attend elementary school.

Finally, he created the post of Prime Minister, so that people abroad might appreciate the fact that his policy evolved in accordance with the times.

He particularly wanted to be "accepted" by the United States, whose protection he sought, being suspicious of the old European colonialists and also of the Soviet Union. It was impossible for him not to have diplomatic relations with the latter, because of the help it had given against fascism, but the Soviet social regime obviously scared him. The Emperor didn't feel safe until he had made his country Washington's most loyal military ally in Africa.

As far as the economy was concerned, the postwar period was distinguished for a process that the 1974 Revolution had to put a stop to at once. Feudal Ethiopia opened its doors to foreign capital, particularly from the United States.

Haile Selassie was trying to build a permanent connection with the West, to save himself from the upheavals that Nasser's rebellion had given rise to in the region, and later from the revolutions breaking out from Vietnam to Cuba, at a time when the USSR and the rest of the socialist world were growing in importance and when ideas concerning far-reaching social change were shaking the so-called Third World.

All of this set off a paradoxical process not unknown in history: Haile Selassie was misunderstood all down the line and criticized by "right" and left. The surrender of military bases to the United States and the facilities provided to encourage it to bring in its dollars and its "way of life" created discontent among the most aristocratic social circles and among the poorest of the poor.

The current of fresh air encouraged by the timid but undeniable increase of capitalism had allowed for the emergence of Marxist ideas among some intellectuals and students, and had objectively made it easier for protest actions to develop among the most oppressed masses, which irritated the nobility. Of course, both phenomena bore the seal of spontaneity and didn't go beyond a struggle against the immediate enemy: master or landowner. The state, at the service of the exploiting classes, went unchallenged, and its absolute chief even more so. The more conservative elements didn't like having their power whittled away by foreign competitors and preferred to keep on "shuffling along" in the old way, without too much modernization in the forms of exploitation. Moreover, the Coptic Church didn't much care for the idea of allowing other practicing religions, such as the Protestant religions which predominate in the United States.

A real pro at doing a balancing act, Haile Selassie always knew the right words to fit the circumstances. In the League of Nations he had been famed for his pronouncements against fascism, which undoubtedly stemmed from the fact that it was in his interest to fight it, as the Ethiopian people were doing with such heroism. Although in defending that kind of an Ethiopia they were defending the ruling regime that suffocated, crushed and stultified the mass of their people. During the postwar period, Haile Selassie built up his empire, giving it certain trimmings of formal democracy. His active postwar foreign policy was of the same style. While granting bases to the country that was following in the footsteps of fascism with its anti-Sovietism and the worldwide crusade against communism, Haile Selassie tried to cloak his treason by making Addis Ababa the headquarters of the Organization of African Unity, and the imperial government presented itself as nonaligned, a lover of peace and even progressive.

When all the demagogic whitewash is removed, it can be seen that the minimal economic growth achieved under Haile Selassie took place in exchange for important concessions to imperialist capital. The United States and West Germany received concessions that allowed them to prospect for and extract oil for half a century in Ethiopia, especially in Ogaden. The entire rare minerals mining industry also fell into foreign hands. The same thing happened to communications and air and land transportation. Virtually all of its industry was divided up among various foreign powers: the sugar industry went to Holland, textiles to Great Britain and Belgium, the chemical industry to Japan, and energy to France. In short, Ethiopia, a feudal country with an embryonic form of capitalism, became neo-colonialized. Soon it was deep in debt, with no real prospects for development.

Out of a total population of 30 million, there weren't even 200,000 workers in Ethiopia.

The Emperor took great pride in having created a national banking system. In fact, the only thing he took back from the British, when they were forced to withdraw in 1954, was the banking concession they had obtained in 1905. Menelik II had introduced the first paper currency in 1915, through the so-called Bank of Abyssinia, but Haile Selassie's national mint not only printed currency bearing his picture surrounded by typical Ethiopian flora and fauna—the Revolution did away with these bills—but also allowed him to amass a fortune and bank it in Switzerland; the exact amount isn't known, but it is undoubtedly one of the largest ever amassed by any one individual.

As a consequence, right from the start, the Revolution had to be not only antifeudal but also anti-imperialist and against the bureaucratic bourgeoisie.

4 A Glance at the Revolution

I

THE REVOLUTION that overthrew Haile Selassie stands in sharp contrast to him.

When Mengistu Haile Mariam once again explained the reasons why the Revolution took place, this time on the third anniversary of its victory, in the square that had at once been renamed Revolution Square, he said, "The fact that the Ethiopian economy lacked a base and was mocked everywhere served to open the way for struggle. The other factor that helped bring on the Revolution was the awakening of the broad masses to Ethiopia's political, economic and social shortcomings and to the fact that all the sources of profit and wealth were owned by the feudal lords and those connected with them through self-interest and personal gain."

Later on he emphasized, "The world knows that it isn't easy to overthrow a monarchy that has lasted 3,000 years. Nor was it easy to suppress the feudal lords, who had consolidated their power over the years, and the bourgeoisie, which had vested interests in power and authority. The task of dismantling the monarchical rule and its countless reactionary hangers-on, who were both astute and politically on the ball, required a hard struggle, but the broad masses of Ethiopia had learned what kind of fight they would have to put up in order to overthrow monarchical rule, and they had also learned that the united force of the oppressed masses could demolish the consolidated ranks of reaction. Here I would like to emphasize the point that this Revolution pertains to no one individual, group or segment in particular. The Revolution belongs to the oppressed masses. Therefore, there can be no conflict among us over who was the first to promote the Revolution and be credited by history as such."

Then he added, "Having uprooted and dismantled the old order that was the source of oppression, our Revolution hasn't fallen prey to somnambulism. It has a definite purpose and objective, which guides the broad oppressed masses and protects their basic interests. Its guiding principle is Marxism-Leninism, the beacon of hope for all oppressed peoples."

The basic factors which contributed to the volcanic eruption of this Revolution that took the world by surprise, precisely because in the contemporary atlas of social struggles there seemed to be no volcano in this zone, may be summed up as

1. the spiraling cost of living;
2. the abominable system of land tenure;
3. the sudden spread of hunger, which became a famine, particularly in Wollo Province;
4. the sudden loss of political control by the authorities, leaving the country with no effective government;
5. the spontaneous uprising of the mass of workers and peasants and city intellectuals against the feudal-bourgeois regime; and
6. the realization by members of the armed forces that they were a part of the people rather than a tool for oppression.

To this day, Ethiopia is an exceptional case in that the general social crisis not only became a crisis within the armed forces but made of them a factor for its solution. On many other occasions, from Nasser's Egypt to el-Qaddafi's Libya (though el-Qaddafi was a political conspirator who deliberately joined the army in order to plot against the power of reaction),

nd including Peru and Portugal, the armed forces
ave been the pivotal point for anti-oligarchic
hange.

However, there are two aspects of the Ethiopian
situation which are worth noting. First, it was not a
military but a people's revolution, a mass, spon-
aneous revolution, to which the armed forces gave
direction in the absence of a revolutionary party or
movement. Second, this factor, far from diminishing,
holding back or detracting from the Revolution or
disregarding the masses, has led to a deeper, broader
revolution, to more participation by the people, to
having the proletariat set up its dictatorship in alliance with the peasants, to uniting military and
civilian revolutionaries within a Marxist-Leninist
Party that provides the kind of general staff that all
revolutions need.

Of course, not all the commanding officers in the
armed forces approved of this road at heart; but, dur-
ng the early days, none dared to go in search of
another road, because the collapse of the old order had
been such that there was no alternative to joining the
revolution of the masses or being swept away by it.

The inevitable process of every class finding its
own level was soon to take place. Spínolas are not
made by wearing haughty monocles or by virtue of
their colonialist, fascist mentality. Their distinguish-
ng feature is that they represent the interests of the
ruling classes.

General Andom was made chief army commander
because the Emperor and all the powerful financiers,
the landholders and the church approved of him. He
could just as easily have become a banker, a noble-
man or a bishop.

The case of Teferi Bente, his successor as President
of the PMAC, who was also executed for treason, was
somewhat different in form but not in essence. Bente
even went so far as to espouse the socialist transformation of the Revolution, but he developed a tremen-

dous personal ambition for power, as well as a na tionalistic point of view and a fear that the people would demand not only that there be more and more profound and rapid change but that he become the protagonist of victory. Teferi Bente thus came to work with the CIA and other secret services (there are documents to prove this) to stage a coup on February 3, 1977, at 9:00 in the morning. The true revolution aries, headed by Mengistu, were one step ahead of them, effecting a countercoup, just one hour earlier that saved the country tremendous bloodshed and safeguarded the popular nature and direction of the Revolution.

In both cases, of course, the plotting leader had his group of followers, and these, too, had to be curbed by revolutionary justice.

Ethiopia becomes less of a unique case if the peas ant problem is properly analyzed; in this, Ethiopia comes closer to a prerevolutionary France than to Africa.

José Pérez Novoa, the first Cuban Ambassador in Addis Ababa, has written in an unpublished work:

> In Africa, colonial domination imposed fron tiers—which, for the colonialists, were the boundaries of their areas of domination—and baptized them with the name of state. Neverthe less, these boundaries didn't really define states in accordance with the existing population, nor were any efforts made to create national homo geneity. The more powerful advanced as far as their forces permitted against their colonialist opponents. The lines of demarcation, then, were the frontiers of domination; they didn't take into consideration the nationality or tribe inhabiting the area. As a consequence, a given nationality or tribe might be split up in the areas that were parceled out, which were called countries.
>
> In the economic field, the colonial system didn't integrate the inhabitants of a country in a common development plan but rather main-

tained the socio-economic formation characteristic of each tribe. Most of these tribes had a self-sufficient form of life and, hence, had no connection with capitalist trade relations. Throughout colonial rule, tribal individuality, the tribal structure, was uppermost; there was no feeling of being an integral part of that superimposed state or nation. Their state, their nation, is the ethnic group to which they belong. Above all, they are Bacongos, Fulas, etc.

It's even very difficult to define a peasant, because this concept can't be based only on living in the countryside; many Africans reap what they consume, but their place in economic production isn't that of a peasant.

To sum up, colonial rule superimposed its structure of domination on African ethnic development, neither destroying nor developing it further, but simply freezing it in time.

Ethiopia is something else. The same author writes:

This country had a state structured to serve a national ruling class, the product of a long historical process. Starting in the last century, the Amharics gradually conquered all the other nationalities and set up a structure of state domination, with all its state bodies. During the three years following the February, 1974, triumph, the struggle necessarily had to be defined in class terms.

What was happening in Ethiopia was that the peasant masses and workers, the oppressed people, were fighting against the ruling feudal class and its state apparatus; first and foremost, then, it was a struggle between oppressors and oppressed within a national framework. This is one of the reasons why the Ethiopian Revolution had a sharp concept of the class struggle and possibly why it developed into one of the fiercest class battles in all the African continent.

What may be observed when analyzing the workers' struggle?

The proletariat has participated right from the start in the Ethiopian Revolution, in spite of the fact that it is relatively small in number. The isolated, craft-based strikes of the past, which were a challenge to the system, were a source of encouragement to the students, and, when the general situation began to deteriorate in 1974, they constituted an undisputed element of radicalization. It is true that there are only 200,000 workers in the processing industries; in textiles, leather, shoes and food; in communications and transportation (the taxi drivers may be said to have triggered the Revolution); and in construction, but they all took part in the spontaneous general strikes in February 1974.

The astonished official trade union leaders, loyal to the Emperor, first tried to lead the workers like sheep along the road of reform; but in the end, as in the case of the officers in the armed forces, they themselves were swept along by the uncontrollable wave of popular insurrection. The working class soon produced new leaders, and it wasn't by chance that the two really revolutionary leaders who had the trust of the masses once union democracy had been won, and both of whom served as General Secretary were assassinated by the counterrevolution.

The students have been an important ally of the workers and peasants. A movement emerged from their ranks in the '60s whose watchword was "Land to the Tillers"; it was this movement that started putting pressure on Parliament, which at the time was discussing a timid agrarian reform such as could only be expected from a preeminently feudal government.

Whenever there had been peasant revolts (in Bale, Sidamo, Gojam, Wollo and particularly Eritrea), the students of Addis Ababa and Asmara had taken to the streets in open protest against the way the revolts were put down.

The May 1968, events in France, in which many Ethiopian scholarship students in Paris took part, added fuel to the fire. Practically all the members of the small underground Marxist groups, most of which were cut off from the working class, came from the students. These groups were reminiscent of the early Marxist groups in Russia at the end of the 19th century, before Lenin brought them and the proletariat together to create a new kind of party.

There is one essential difference though. In 1900, St. Petersburg had large concentrations of industrial workers, whereas Addis Ababa in 1974 did not. In spite of this, Lenin had pointed out that, as a whole, Russia under the czars suffered not so much from capitalist development as from its insufficient development. Equally czarist Ethiopia was suffering from an amazing (for our day and age) development of feudalism. On March 14, during his visit to Ethiopia only six weeks after the revolutionary leaders had removed the treacherous rightists from power, Fidel correctly said that the Ethiopian Revolution was a mixture of the French and Bolshevik Revolutions.

With regard to the students, more and more of them are coming to take an active part in the revolutionary process, but there is no doubt that they, too, are going through a process of class polarization, much like the one within the armed forces.

It must be remembered that only aristocratic, feudal, capitalist families had been able to send their children to secondary school, not to speak of the university, either in Addis Ababa or abroad. Moreover, Pérez Novoa also brings out another factor: "As opposition to Haile Selassie was taking root, the main repressive force was the army: this meant that there was soon a clear antagonistic contradiction between the army and the students. Since it is the army that is carrying the main weight of the present revolutionary process, subjectively there is a large, hard-to-bridge abyss between students and leaders."

It should also be noted that a great many students have adopted an entrenched antimilitarist stance, one that could only be justified if the armed forces had taken the side of the oppressors; in effect, because of this, many students have themselves ended up on the side of the oppressors, whether or not they want to admit it. The so-called Ethiopian People's Revolutionary Party (EPRP), that engages in counterrevolutionary terrorism in the cities, originally drew its ranks from the students. As was only to be expected, they had a source of inspiration in Maoism. For fear of joining the military, who only yesterday were at the service of reaction, and failing to understand that the army today serves the Revolution, these former students have fallen into the hands of ousted landowners and into the network of plots engineered against the Ethiopian Revolution by international imperialism and Arab reaction. Of course, also present is the petty bourgeoisie's loathing of discipline, organization and giving way to the masses—even though it invokes their name at all times as the principal driving force in history.

One must not exaggerate, however. The truth is that more and more students are joining the Revolution, and more will do so as more children of workers and peasants become students, an opportunity they didn't have before. Also, life itself shows honest students on which side the Revolution stands, and on which side the counterrevolution. Thirdly, the hateful actions sponsored by the leaders of the EPRP, such as the murder of workers' leaders, have opened the eyes of many who had been taken in. All this explains the recent split within the EPRP, with the appearance of a wing that is abandoning counterrevolution.

Almost as soon as the Revolution came to power in December 1974, the National Work Campaign Program was launched. Some 60,000 high school and university students, teachers and soldiers were sent to rural areas to teach the poor, stultified masses how to read and write and to organize them in peasant associations. Their mission was also to teach something decisive in Ethiopia: the alphabet of all revolutions—that is, how to distinguish between friendly and enemy classes, between revolutionary and counterrevolutionary forces.

The principal motto of the campaign is an antidote to petty bourgeois bragging: "Learn from the masses and, in turn, teach the masses."

The author has met many of those who took part in the campaign who have said that this was how they became Marxist-Leninists.

5 Roots of Spontaneity

TO UNDERSTAND more clearly why the surprising explosion of February 1974 occurred, it is useful to have an overview of Ethiopia's very complicated history.

The first thing to point out is that it was the only African state that managed to remain independent in the period when the great capitalist powers entered the stage of imperialism and finished dividing up the world, at the end of the 19th century.

There were numerous attempts to cut up and control Ethiopia, but the people's armed struggle in an isolated, mountainous area made it possible to preserve Ethiopian state independence. Only Eritrea—a kind of cap over Ethiopia's head, with two ports providing access to the sea—wound up being set apart at that time. It fell to Italy, which gave it that name in 1890.

Ethiopia's history has been truly complex. Between 300 and 570 B.C., the Ethiopians ruled southern Arabia. History changed that equation. In the last quarter of the 6th century A.D., the Arabs invaded and conquered all of the Middle East, northern Africa and southern Europe. They ruled for 11 centuries. In the first quarter of the 16th century, their empire declined and collapsed. It then became a bone of contention between Turkey and Portugal, rivals at opposite ends of the Mediterranean, whose confrontation took place in the Middle East and the Indian Ocean, directly threatening Ethiopia.

Turkish forces began their march to the Red Sea in 1520. Some 50 years later (in 1572), the Ottoman Khedive, who ruled Egypt and controlled the port of Mesewa, near Asmara, established garrisons on the low-lying western coast. When the Khedive's forces were beaten by the Ethiopians at Gundet three years later and that victory was repeated at Gura in 1576, the Turks decided to withdraw. However, another sword was poised over the country, held by Italy.

With the imperialist era of world history openly under way by 1896—coinciding with the Cubans' final war against Spain and against US intervention aimed at taking over Cuba, Puerto Rico and the Philippines, whose peoples were also fighting for independence— Italy pounced on Ethiopia.

The famous Battle of Adwa saved the Ethiopians from falling under Italian domination. Ethiopian patriots have always found a source of encouragement against foreign aggression in Adwa.

Almost 40 years later, Mussolini tried to wipe out that defeat by occupying the whole country.

On December 5, 1934, in Ogaden, near the reservoir of the Wal Wal Oasis, some 100 kilometers from another traditional border, that of Somalia, which was then an Italian colony, Rome's troops clashed with those of Addis Ababa, but it was only a minor border incident involving the passage of caravans.

However, Mussolini whipped up passions to fever pitch with his bellowed boasts from his famous balcony on the Piazza Venezia in Rome; and, having infected the entire Italian nation with chauvinism, he refused to apply the arbitration measures provided in the 1928 Treaty that the League of Nations had sponsored for solving problems between the two countries. Rome immediately demanded that the Wal Wal Oasis be added to its colonial territories in Somalia.

Italy sought to annex western Ethiopia in order to consummate its long-time project of a railroad to link its possessions in Ethiopia and in Somalia. Here it rivaled France, mistress of the port of Djibouti and of the Djibouti-Addis Ababa railroad. Fascist Rome had sought an alliance with London in order to confront Paris, and this was agreed to in 1925. For their part, the British wanted permission to build a dam on the Blue Nile, at Lake Tana, and a highway linking the dam area with the Sudan. Thus, British imperialism would be the major beneficiary of the economy of the Nile basin countries.

At that time the Parisian Foreign Minister was Pierre Laval, an open servant of the Nazis, who didn't hesitate to sign an accord with Mussolini in 1935, a month after the incident at the Wal Wal Oasis occurred. Laval, in turn, wanted Italy to help him soften the sharpening contradictions France had with Nazi Germany. In return for French support, Italy renounced its claims to Tunisia and other French colonies. Meanwhile, Rome received 20 percent of the stock in the Djibouti-Addis Ababa railroad line and the eagerly sought certainty (by secret agreement) that France would back its conquest of Ethiopia.

Entire nations were shamefully and cynically carved up before the eyes of the world. Britain declared herself indifferent to the Ethiopian situation as long as her rights to Lake Tana were recognized (she was equally indifferent, later on, to the plot against the Spanish Republic). The US Congress adopted a similar position with its passage of the Neutrality Act in August 1935, which forbade the sale of arms to both aggressor and victim. Ethiopia's fate was sealed.

The Soviet Union was the only country that clearly and firmly supported the independence of Ethiopia (then called Abyssinia) and world peace, which was seriously threatened by the conflict.

Under these circumstances, Mussolini declared that the Italian-Abyssinian problem had ceased to be a "diplomatic conflict" and had become a "historic" conflict—whose solution required "the use of arms."

On the night of October 2, 1935, Italian troops stationed in Eritrea and Somalia invaded Ethiopia. Haile Selassie's government urgently asked the League of Nations for help. On the 7th, thanks to the USSR's staunch position, the League was forced to conclude that Mussolini's government had resorted to war, in violation of the provisions of Article 12 of the 1928 League Convention, and called for the imposition of sanctions, as provided in Article 16. The sanctions were never applied, however, for all the imperialist powers joined in sabotaging any such attempt.

On December 9, British and French Foreign Ministers Hoare and Laval proposed a new plan for solving the problem. It couldn't have been worse: that Ethiopia cede to Italy the western part of Ogaden and the area between Ogaden and Eritrea—Danakil and Tigre. In "compensation," Ethiopia was offered the Eritrean port of Aseb—at a previously established high price! Of course, London could lend it the money, provided the Ethiopian economy fell graciously into its hands. As if the spoils weren't enough, central Ethiopia, including the capital, would be placed under the control of League of Nations "advisers" designated by Britain, France and Italy. Ethiopia, naturally, refused to commit suicide.

In the face of the crime thus perpetrated, the USSR and people throughout the world mobilized to aid the poorly armed African state then under attack. Committees for the Defense of Ethiopia appeared in many countries, particularly in Africa. Volunteer battalions were organized in South Africa, Egypt and Syria, as was a Support Committee from among Black trade unionists of the United States.

The Communist International had foreseen—in Dimitrov's and Togliatti's reports to its 7th Congress—that fascism would move to open aggression and had called for a united front and action. Now, it threw itself into the passionate defense of Ethiopia.

Meanwhile, Mussolini got the backing of the Catholic Church, which in that period was very sympahetic to colonial interests in Africa and Asia. The Vatican also hoped that an Italian victory would lead the dissident Coptic Church to return to the fold. Cardinal Idelfonso Schuster [Milan] described the war as "a national and a Catholic mission."

The Ethiopian people rallied with real patriotism to the just struggle for independence. The heroism of the barefoot masses who fought with lances, foreshadowed that of the Spanish, who fell victim to fascism shortly thereafter. However, with only a few guns, no central military command and fighting on two fronts—north and south, Ethiopia couldn't hold out. Its regular army was small, and regional recruitment was extremely hurried and was handled by the ras, whom the people detested for their abuses as landowners.

Superiority in weapons, uncontested control of the air and the use of asphyxiating poisonous gases gave fascist Italy a fairly easy victory. For example, in the battle of Azebo Galla, Mussolini lost 100 soldiers, while Ethiopia lost nearly 20,000. Another negative factor for the Ethiopians was their poor military leadership. Haile Selassie refused to change tactics, even when it was impossible to withstand the Italian assault. He wouldn't listen when his military advisers urged going to the mountains and waging a stubborn, mobile, guerrilla war.

On May 5, 1936, General Badoglio sent Mussolini a telegram announcing the seizure of Addis Ababa, Harer and Dire Dawa. Military superiority had been coupled with treason on the part of Haile Selassie Gugsa, the Emperor's son-in-law and rival.

On May 9, Mussolini announced to the Great Council of Fascism, with his customary theatrical pose, "Ethiopia is Italian! Italian in fact and in law. With the population of Ethiopia, peace is a foregone conclusion. The new Emperor of Ethiopia is King Victor Emmanuel."

On June 30, the League of Nations reviewed the

Ethiopian Government's motion against recognizing the Italian conquest. Only the USSR supported it. There were 23 votes against and 25 abstentions.

Mussolini immediately wanted to send half a million Italians to work the mines and fertile lands of the new possessions of the "Italian East Africa Empire" in order to secure the conquest. He also sought to make Ethiopia a stategic base, but the plan had to be abandoned because the Ethiopians went on fighting even long after all the members of the imperial government had left.

The fascist occupation was as brutal as could be expected. More than 400,000 Ethiopians were murdered, 300,000 died of hunger, and 35,000 perished in concentration camps.

The Italian colonial authorities also resorted to all kinds of intrigue and maneuvers in their efforts to dominate the Ethiopian people. They incited the Tigres and Galas against the Amharas, and the Somalis against the Danakils; they fomented discord between Muslims and Christians, made thousands of promises, etc.

All to no avail. After five years of heroic, constant resistance, the partial occupation was defeated as the Allied troops carried forward their East Africa offensive. The basic factor in the liberation, however, was the struggle of the Ethiopian peasant guerrillas. Addis Ababa was liberated on May 5, 1941, and there were no invaders left in the country by the end of the year. The loss of Ethiopia marked the beginning of the end for Mussolini's regime and dealt a severe blow to the global strategy of the Rome-Berlin-Tokyo Axis.

For Ethiopia however, and particularly for its people, the victory over the fascist invaders didn't mean real independence. Britain sought to take advantage of the presence of her troops, as an allied force, to become a new occupier, and, in spite of the Ethiopian

Government's protests, the British remained until 1954.

This prolonged battle explains the Ethiopian people's patriotism, that has been magnified by their Revolution.

6 The Work of the Revolution

RIDICULING the fencing among exploiting ruling class heads and parties, lords of the land and of banking, in mid-19th-century Europe—before communism, like a specter filled with reality, brought the proletariat's defiant face on stage—Marx wrote, "The so-called revolutions of 1848 were nothing but small episodic events, slight fractures and fissures in the hard crust of European society. However, they were sufficient to show the abyss that lay below. They demonstrated that, beneath that surface, so solid in appearance, there were veritable oceans that had only to start moving to make entire continents break up into bits of hard rock."

That same analysis is applicable to 20th-century Africa.

If the most honest plebiscite had been conducted in Ethiopia in 1970, the Emperor would undoubtedly have had his immense power ratified. With very few exceptions, all the people not only believed in him blindly but adored him.

This was the fruit of centuries of feudalism, during which very few advances were made in the means of production, while progressive social ideas penetrated even more slowly. It was also the result of systematic propaganda, designed with the most modern publicity techniques and aimed at deceiving the masses and preventing them from thinking for themselves, leaving everything up to the Emperor.

Although his absurdities, whims and abuses—visited even on his children and close followers—weren't always easily swallowed by the more Europeanized elements of the two ruling classes, the latifundists and bureacratic capitalists, they accepted Haile Selassie and promoted his myth because it provided the surest guarantee anywhere in Africa against the revolutionary changes advocated following the death of fascism and, with it, of the old colonial system.

Suddenly, all that submission went down the drain. The masses stopped believing in the Emperor and began to believe in themselves. Without an oppressed class that could take command, without even factions of it grouped in parties or movements, there was a vacuum. Only the army could fill it, and that was when the other characteristic emerged—which, as much as the spontaneity, evokes admiration and also apprehension for present-day Ethiopia.

It is interesting and worthwhile to analyze this characteristic—the military factor.

For a long time, the question of what the army could do in power was a legitimate one.

Now, today, it is a matter of analyzing what it has done.

Naturally, just as the means of production are nothing without people, even automatic machines need someone to dream them up, build them and introduce them in the creative process, so the Ethiopian people have been and are behind the army.

Gradually, the people are replacing the army as the Revolution's most decisive element. Ethiopia is becoming more and more "civilian."

This means that peasants and workers, a majority of the urban petty bourgeoisie and certain middle-level sectors of the bourgeoisie, as well as many intellectuals, have become the true protagonists, in a conscious and organized manner, of the Revolution.

The army hasn't returned to its garrisons. Not only is it fighting on the eastern border against the invaders, or defending Asmara against the blows of the separatist forces encouraged by the Arab reaction and imperialism, but it is also developing the consciousness that it belongs to the people and must serve them.

A marvelous process of revolutionizing soldiers and command cadres is taking place in the midst of the Revolution. Urban and field workers come en masse to the training centers and join the militia, now the basic defense force. The militiamen go to the trenches with minimal training in handling weapons and fight alongside their brothers, the professional soldiers.

The same thing is true with respect to the economy, education and the law.

As "boys with new shoes," the masses, feverish with the joy of feeling more than free—masters—organize, discuss, study, learn, lead—and ignore no aspect of social life, for none is beyond their scope.

What has happened?

It was also Marx who discovered: "In all manifestations that are disconcerting to the bourgeoisie, to the aristocracy and to the poor prophets of regression, we recognize our good friend Robin Goodfellow, the old mole who knows how to excavate the earth so quickly, that worthy sapper called Revolution."

There are the allegedly dispassionate observers who, offhandedly and without having been in Ethiopia since February 1974, still believe it to be in the midst of the social chaos that existed at the time the old regime fell or in the subsequent period of high-level coups and countercoups.

There's no point in asking them what they want. From the French Revolution to the revolution that may be taking place right now, anywhere, that is always the rule rather than the exception.

However, if violence persists and increases in Ethiopia, the guilty ones are the enemies of its popular revolution.

The Chile of heroic Allende didn't set its sights so high—by a long shot—as Ethiopia does, and imperialism and the ruling classes didn't hesitate to resort to extremely savage methods to strangle it.

South Africa and Rhodesia have broken all records in the Olympics of Crime.

The number of traitorous ministers and generals that Ethiopia's revolutionary courts have had to send before the firing squad in three years—to prevent Andom from becoming a Pinochet, or a fascist regime such as Pretoria's or Salisbury's from setting itself up in Addis Ababa—is insignificant compared to the number of peasants the landlords murdered in a single month—and continued doing so for decades—when their Emperor held absolute, final and almighty power.

As for the lies about massacres of 500 students a day, presented by the capitalist press in New York and Paris as coming from "reliable sources," I have heard US and French diplomats in Addis Ababa deplore the fact that the press could have considered such stupidities credible.

It is true that there has been sporadic crossfire, in which one or two terrorists, not to mention a *kebele* militiaman or policeman, died. However, the Revolution is not to blame; this is the work of the counter-revolution.

Human loss in the city and countryside will disappear as the new democratic-revolutionary state of workers and peasants is consolidated. As far as others are concerned, the university has reopened, and 80 percent of its students, at a conservative estimate, are enrolled.

Neither social chaos nor bloodbath. Ethiopia is chiefly the mirror of something else: a genuine revolution.

Marx spoke in poetic language of "veritable oceans" that suddenly begin to move: the masses. The "hard rock" they break up are the social injustices that deprive them of freedom, dignity, land, food, shoes and other clothing, health and hope.

The Revolution has made more changes in Ethiopia in just three years than were previously made in three millennia.

A list of the chief gains the masses have won thus far is impressive, though they aren't the most important from the point of view of future perspectives. Those will include overcoming the abysmal underdevelopment, industrializing, increasing well-being, and forging a new, educated and advanced Ethiopia.

It is impossible to draw up a list of its achievements, because how do you measure the feeling of equality?

II

The Ethiopian Revolution's first act was to depose Haile Selassie and end his regime of absolute feudal monarchy.

The fall of the Bourbons heralded for the French the possibility to develop the modern nation of France.

For Ethiopia, such a process has an even deeper meaning.

Any analysis must start from the fact that Ethiopia had official, marginal slavery up to 1950; until just three years ago, it had arrogant feudalism, with latifundists who owned areas larger than the island of Cuba.

It must also be considered that, in the third quarter of the atomic and space flight century, the belief that the Emperor ruled "by divine right" was not only accepted by the masses; it was the only concept that could enter minds closed by a total fanaticism imparted almost like a family heritage and reinforced by sermons from the cradle to the grave.

Up to February 1974, Ethiopians viewed Haile Selassie as the nearest thing to a god, immune to human foibles, egoism, greed and cowardice.

Any number of philosopher-novelists have described the kind of cataclysm that occurs in the minds of many believers who, through a better understanding of nature, come to feel that "God is dead." Sometimes it isn't easy to find the road leading to that new conviction—which, in any case, isn't absolutely necessary in order to struggle against social evils.

What could have led Haile Selassie's 30 million idolizers to lose confidence in him, deny him, scorn him and hate him with as much force as they had previously adored him?

In a single night, millions of pictures of "God's Elected" were set on fire by the same hands that had formerly touched the ground he walked on, as the subject knelt. The same eyes that once shone with tears when the supreme face appeared in the distance burned as they watched the flames turn to ashes the image that was now a symbol of evil and hypocrisy.

Something much more intense than a flame must have kindled in the soul of the Ethiopians. It's easy to say "consciousness," but, in addition to making such ignorant and ignored people understand it, how was it possible to make each one feel it for himself, discover it on his own, amidst the tangled thicket of prejudice and obscurantism?

I had a very revealing experience. I asked a night watchman—one of those who has guarded a building for 20, 24 or 30 years—who made him believe in the Revolution when he used to believe in the Emperor? And this watchman, with skin as black and lined as a campaign boot, answered, "Nobody."

Then, apparently fearing I wouldn't believe his change was a sincere one, he corrected himself and exclaimed, "Everybody!"

That is the secret!

That is, the disbelief in the myth, the detoxification, happened in the only way possible: at the same time, for everybody.

With their collective awakening synchronized by

errible blows that made class identification possible,
all the peasants understood that hunger was the result not of the earth's lack of water but of the latifundist's existence and that the latifundist to beat all
atifundists was the Emperor.

The taxi drivers, the railroad, telegraph and public
office workers, the newspaper peddlers, and the unemployed, all suddenly saw that the worst culprit was
he one they had thought of as father and friend.

He was a semidevil, not a semigod.

Then the shouts of "Down with the Emperor!"
which might once have come from bold students at the
entrance to the University, ceased being the voice of
evil and madness and became the voice of goodness,
ruth and reason.

It is impossible to determine who was the first
Ethiopian to become a revolutionary between February and September 1974. It must have happened to
many at the same time.

When the wave began to pound at the garrisons, and
the soldiers and policemen began to form committees,
as the workers and peasants had done, and to present
their demands for wage increases—and especially
when the officers joined in the spontaneous protest
action—those who still believed in Haile Selassie
became the defeated members of a silent minority.

The highly complex question of consciousness-
raising, which undoubtedly had a thousand and one
variations, can be illustrated by what I was told by
someone who is now a colonel and an important person in the process.

He explained to me that, one day in March 1974, he
learned that a commission had been created in his
unit to demand higher wages to meet escalating prices. He decided to say nothing and pretend not to
notice.

Nevertheless, he immediately found himself
among the privates and sergeants selected in mass
meetings to present the demands at the Ministry of

Defense office, in view of the fact that the commissioned officers had adopted an attitude of singular neutrality.

Actually, nobody could or would demand that "legal channels" be used, and the word "insubordination" had been practically eliminated from the language for several weeks. During that period thousands of people rushed to join street demonstrations at all hours of the day, now without police or military patrols.

Nevertheless, the commissioned officers didn't take to the demands—which would have benefited them, as well.

Nothing was said in the Ministry of Defense, so someone—Mengistu?—suggested going directly to see the Emperor. And here history becomes still more revealing and sensational. As if he had been expecting them, the Emperor received them himself.

The sentry at a side door (the small group didn't dare go to the front door) merely advised the head of the palace guard of their presence, and he, in turn, immediately took the thorny question—which only a short time earlier would have been no less absurd than seeing the Emperor sweep the streets or beg for alms—to the highest level.

The colonel told me they all shouted, "Long live the Emperor!" when he came in, as in the military parade held on his ascent to the throne a half century earlier. Then, encouraged by the Emperor's paternal smile, they articulated their request.

"It's impossible, Your Majesty, to live on the wages we are getting. You have been betrayed. The soldiers are poorly paid, and veterans' pensions have been eliminated."

"Be calm, my soldiers. We, God's Elected, understand you. We will take care of everything."

Right there, during the meeting, Haile Selassie ordered that the soldiers' wages be raised by 10 percent, and the officers' by 5. Naturally, the "Long live the

Emperor!" that followed was the loudest ever heard, and the sincerity of those who shouted it seemed unquestionable.

However, prices began to soar even higher, which prompted the soldiers to visit the Emperor a second time.

This time he smiled less, but he enunciated another "We, God's Elected," and the promise of another wage increase.

Three weeks later, a totally different scene took place, when the Fourth Division Committee appeared, not only with its own demands but also with those of sectors—the teachers, railroad workers and small businessmen—none of whom had been received by their respective ministers, much less by the Emperor. With an outward show of exaggerated patience, while bridling with ill-concealed ire, Haile Selassie said, "How much more? *I* don't have any more money. I can't go on paying wage hikes. The last one came out of *my own pocket*."

The colonel told me that the "Long live the Emperor!" at the end of that interview was a murmur—or a curse—and that everyone—the Emperor, the servants who were present and all the members of the Committee—interpreted it as such.

As far as the colonel is concerned, when he heard "I" rather than "We, God's Elected," and that business of "my own pocket," that was the end.

"Quite simply, I began to hate him."

III

Once Haile Selassie was deposed from the soul of the people and from his throne, then what?

Then and there, the unanimity within the social forces that had fostered or accepted the bloodless overthrow of the Emperor was broken.

Particularly dramatic and decisive was the differentiation that began to take place almost auto-

matically within the force that removed that century-
old obstacle from the road to Ethiopia's historical
development. The army, the only institution operating, began to break up into rival factions.

There is no doubt that personal aspirations explain
the immediate reasons why any general, colonel or
captain followed a particular line and joined one of
the many groups that began to operate politically
within the military, operating as a balance force precisely because of its alleged apoliticism. At a time
when the entire hierarchy—starting at the very top—
is crumbling, it is logical that the military should
replace "I obey" with "I command." But, when all is
said and done, there were also reasons for this attitude.

Personal ambition was induced by or identified
with class ambition. General Andom not only wanted
to be the Bonapartist dictator of the young revolution
but also felt the greatest repugnance for the idea that
private ownership of land, finances and factories
should disappear. He was horrified to think that a
popular, socialist Ethiopia might emerge from the
Ethiopian convulsion.

General Andom's blue blood curdled in his veins
when he heard his captains speak, in the meetings
called at any hour in the garrisons, of the need to
study Marx and Lenin. For him, with his indoctrina-
tion from Washington, it was clear that this meant the
beginning of the century's terrible epidemic that was
leading to the death of the sacred right to own the
wealth produced by other hands and other human
lives.

Why, then, was Andom at the head of the Provisional Military Administrative Council?

The explanation is very simple. What began spontaneously on February 13 with cries of protest and
then became angry action after learning of the hunger
in the provinces was initially a rebellion, not a revolution. It became a revolution due to its mass force. It

began as something similar to, yet enormously different from, May 1968, in Paris. Haile Selassie wasn't De Gaulle, and this kind of protest doesn't have the same sense and force when it starts in the heart of Europe as when it happens in Africa. Both show up the system's illness, but the feudal system was weaker than the imperialist one—so much so that its institutions fell down like a row of dominoes or a house of cards.

In such a situation, the army had only two alternatives: to smash the protest that was becoming more and more like an uprising—or to join it.

The General Staff chose the latter.

Of course, it tried the former first. In many places, the army repressed demonstrations, strikes and meetings in the usual way. This was another point at which Mengistu showed himself to be not just a captain, but a political leader the Revolution needed.

It was he who pushed the idea of not firing on the people, of supporting their demands as well as those of the military and of setting up committees in the units to do so. This was what led to the creation of the Coordinating Committee of the Army, Police and other military sectors and finally to the formation of the PMAC, ready to become a supreme state body.

Taking great care that the personal ambitions of so many generals and colonels not be attributed to him, Mengistu never opposed the idea of grafting the entire militry hierarchy onto the trunk of the Revolution. With Andom as military chief, he could head the revolutionary process. Wasn't it true that, for months, there were many soldiers—as well as many people from the grass roots— who thought the Emperor himself could head the renovation? Perhaps it would be enough to return spiritually to the days of the Ethiopian Youth movement.

Really, Andom wasn't a traitor—just a deceiver. From the very first, he acted to slow down, weaken, adulterate and, in the end, kill the Revolution.

Immediately after coming to power, he made secret contact with the latifundist party, the Ethiopian Democratic Union (EDU), which, without losing any time, used all the enormous energy that Lenin noticed in the overthrown classes to launch a civil war in response to the Revolution that was trying desperately to be peaceful, nationalist and reasonable.

The EDU hadn't been a strong party when the Emperor was a party all by himself, but, when he fell, it understood that it was now or never and devoted itself to organizing armed detachments of backward peasants with a slave mentality, priests and all kinds of servants to fight, first of all, against the agrarian reform that would inevitably be decreed.

What most annoyed Andom about the agrarian reform was Mengistu's idea of nationalizing the land rather than simply dividing it up—which would whet the appetite of the rural bourgeoisie, who, to a certain extent, would replace the latifundists, so that, in the end, the two classes would join in opposing the Revolution.

Without a doubt, for both Andom and Mengistu, the agrarian problem had become the key and basic question of the Revolution.

In addition to his secret involvement with the EDU, Andom wanted to abolish only certain gross manifestations of feudalism, modernize it and make it bourgeois.

Already holding Marxist-Leninist positions, Mengistu wanted to end the system of feudal exploitation once and for all and prevent the plague of new exploiters from appearing in the countryside.

Mengistu's plans constituted a challenge!

Africa had never known such radicalism. There had been more moderate stages in the Chinese, Vietnamese and Cuban Revolutions, but the only antecedent as drastic in all world history was the agrarian program of the Bolshevik Party in 1917.

Of course, this wasn't just a matter of somebody's

whim. It reflected the depth of the internal class struggle.

For centuries, the Ethiopian peasants had struggled for the land. More than a few latifundists' heads had rolled before the humble, starving workers lost their own. Those isolated successive protests sometimes reached the level of revolts, but never of revolutionary moments. Moreover, the peasants' looks of hatred never encompassed the Emperor. On the contrary, he was their last hope.

Nor was it easy to find formulas for a reform that was to be definitive and applicable throughout the country. The problem to be solved was very complex, very crucial and very involved, because feudalism in Ethiopia was administered in regions, each of which contained more than a hundred different forms of land tenure. A general, uniform revolutionary solution couldn't be found without a concrete regional understanding of the relations of production established among feudalists, agrarian bourgeoisie and peasants of every type and condition. It was very, very difficult.

In the south and most of the central part of the country, more than 85 percent of the rural population lived in the worst circumstances. Barely 10 percent of them had any land at all. In the north and the remaining central part of the country, there was a system based on the age of family members, regulating the use only of the land. This led to its increased fragmentation and the creation of minifarms, supplied to order.

Long lines of peasants bearing petitions, appeals and demands related to the land were to be seen at the entrances to courts all over the country.

Feudalism's design in Ethiopia had certain outlines that existed in many other countries of tropical Africa a century ago, but even then these features were behind the times. In the present century, they couldn't be found anywhere in Latin America, either.

1. Millions of peasants lacked land. This was their fate generation after generation. They owned a bare 5 percent of all the country's arable land.

2. Sixty-five percent of the land was owned by a nobility composed of a handful of families. The most powerful and wealthy, of course, was the Emperor's.

3. Thirty percent of the remaining land belonged to the higher orders of the Orthodox Church of Ethiopia.

4. The main objective of production was consumption rather than the accumulation of capital. This meant that the vast army of peasants constituted a veritable human herd at the level of domestic servants. It didn't matter if they died of hunger. Their mission, decade after decade, was simply to support the extravagant lifestyle of the parasitic oligarchy. This explains why the peasants had to hand over up to three fourths of what they produced with such difficulty.

5. Manacled as a consequence of the fact that 90 percent of the country's population was linked to this type of agriculture, which didn't use fertilizers, chemicals, modern tools or irrigation, the national economy was one of the poorest in the world. Ethiopia was more backward than Haiti, and that's saying a lot. Per capita income (which, with such vast social differences, doesn't reflect the reality) was only $60 a year—less than the $90 figure given by the UN. A few years before the Revolution burst forth, a timid attempt was made to modernize agriculture, but it left very few traces. The imperial government financed projects that favored importing fertilizers and some tractors to raise productivity per area and per man. This meant, of course, that members of the royal family and its few associates who were engaged in the business of producing and exporting coffee were the beneficiaries.

6. Ethiopia exported a great deal of coffee, which provided 60 percent of its foreign exchange income and tied it to the fluctuations of the world market. Year after year, its foreign debt increased. The balance of payments deficit has been chronic for a long time now.

Andom and Mengistu represented the battle between the opposing interests and ideologies of feudalists and peasants.

General Andom's counterrevolutionary plot had to be defeated on November 24, 1974, in order to make possible the historic declaration of March 4, 1975, which abolished the feudal system of land tenure and declared that land was the collective property of all the people.

Land nationalization also included the few modern farms that raised coffee, since most of such rural commercial enterprises were in the hands of the bourgeois latifundists and their allies, the imperialist monopolies and the big Ethiopian bourgeoisie.

Nationalization, however, wasn't enough. It was then necessary to perform the huge task of giving the land to the peasant masses free and clear, so they could put it to work.

At that time, the revolutionary group around Mengistu and Abate—who later turned traitor—conceived the *zemecha* campaign for mobilizing thousands of people—students, teachers and soldiers, all volunteers—to work in the countryside, helping the peasants set up associations and cooperatives. Each family had the right to work ten hectares of land, and every 80 families could establish an association. Peasants who had owned less than ten hectares of land were given additional land to meet that figure and joined the associations if they so desired.

Over 24,000 associations and cooperatives had been created as of September 1977, grouping more than 7 million peasants at the local, district, provincial and regional levels.

Work is now being done to create an All-Ethiopia Peasant Association, which will give the country's nationalities more facilities for exercising regional autonomy.

Through their organizations, established on absolutely democratic bases, the rural masses exercise their political, economic and social rights and are the real owners not only of the land but also of political power.

The peasants' first victory was to eliminate hunger from the countryside. The second, also of interest to the urban population, is that great, collectively worked areas are beginning to appear, and these must produce for commercial exchange. New work and living habits are being created, step by step.

Freed from worry about "where" they'll be exploited, since all exploitation is ended—as is the anguish over lack of land—the peasants base themselves on their associations and cooperatives, looking for better seeds, fertilizers and better work tools.

When you visit an association, however, it isn't just the work done in common that arouses admiration. According to the law, they, the members of an association, can apply the law. There are courts whose judges they elect to rule on minor infractions. They have also had to confront feudal assassins, who have attacked the peasants in their houses by night and burned their stables and their planted fields. Hence, every association and cooperative has its own militia to defend the new revolutionary homeland, now that the land is in their hands.

The highest proof of how democratic the process is lies in the fact that more than 300,000 peasants have joined the militia and the number will soon reach half a million, or a million—as many as may be required for the victory of their Revolution.

The revolutionary power has already trained tens of thousands of these volunteer militiamen and considers the peasants' and workers' militias to be the bulwark of the defense of the country and the Revolution.

IV

In Ethiopia, feudalism also penetrated the cities. The feudal-bourgeois ruling class's ownership of more than 80 percent of the urban land gave it another handle for plundering the masses.

The housing problem was very serious: landlords grabbed a large part of family incomes. The capital and other cities were ringed with slums where indigents lived without water or light, like rats, in garbage dumps.

In addition to the need to find a radical solution to this economic tragedy, a political factor was involved. Since the same people (or their relatives) owned land in the countryside and in the cities, land nationalization led them to use their urban property for counterrevolutionary activities. Thus, there was no alternative but to respond positively to the popular demand for nationalization of urban land and of the "surplus houses"—those not personally inhabited by their owners.

Finally, the PMAC acceded to that demand. Mengistu defended the interests of the poor, opposing those voices of high officers, the sons of landlords, who were against it. And the law appeared, to the people's great joy.

It made city land the property of the nation and reduced house rents by 50 percent. The "surplus houses" became collective property. August 7, 1975, was the day chosen to approve the measure.

When it proceeded to nationalize the urban estates and houses held in reserve, the PMAC discovered things that would have been astonishing had there been any room for astonishment after the discovery of the virtual slave labor that went on in the Emperor's gold mines and of his unparalleled personal fortune stashed away in Switzerland. For it became known that Haile Selassie was the biggest landlord of them all, and that he and the 9 other members of the royal family, 10 high-ranking nobles, 10 very wealthy but non-aristocratic state officials and 20 capitalists owned 2,150 hectares of urban land in the capital alone. This included almost all the houses.

Of that enormous total area, 41 percent was owned by the 10 members of the royal family and 54 percent by the 10 feudal nobles not related to the monarch; the rest was divided among the other big landlords. Only 8 percent of the land was left for a million people. This land had all the low-rent housing located in the outlying areas, with unpaved streets and no sewers—good neighborhoods for the poor.

With great fanfare, the Emperor began expensive urban renewal projects that were really designed to surround the Jubilee Palace with beautiful buildings and avenues, taking into consideration the fact that the Organization of African Unity has its headquarters in Addis Ababa.

But, aside from the prestige, there was the business. Vile and dirty. Contract speculation, collusion for the wealthy, who stuffed themselves with profits until they almost burst. And first and foremost was the demigod, inexplicably concerned with worldly matters.

THERE WAS a profound revolution in the educational system, as well. Its purpose was, first of all, to eliminate feudal and bourgeois ideas and guarantee that scientific socialism would become daily educational fare for those who face the future and must build it.

In Ethiopia, there was still everything to be done in this area. The starting point was even below zero.

A UNESCO study showed that, in 1974, between 95 and 98 percent of the population was illiterate, a figure matched by no other country in Africa or any other part of the world. Of an estimated 8 to 9 million school-aged children, only 500,000 could attend school. Most of these, of course, were in the urban areas. Only 3 of every 1,000 young people over 15 years of age attended any kind of school—and almost all of them, naturally, came from more or less well-off families.

In this panorama, those few students who managed to reach the university level (university enrollment was under 6,000 in the single university in the capital, which had limited facilities and faculty) were trained to become efficient bureaucrats, who identified body and soul with the feudal-capitalist system. To aspire to be a scientist was nothing short of heresy.

In spite of such adverse conditions, the student masses constantly came out against the regime they were supposed to serve, particularly each time the peasants rose up against their bosses.

Thus, the Revolution had to act in many areas, from launching literacy campaigns—in which it ran up against the fact that many of the 80 nationalities and ethnic groups in the country had no alphabets for their spoken languages—to building schools and training teachers.

In the midst of a virtual civil war unleashed by the latifundists, faced with counterrevolutionary terrorism in the cities and fighting regular wars on various fronts, the Revolution carries out its offensive in education.

Spectacular results are out of the question, but there have been admirable and promising gains. The measures concerning educational content are particularly important: no more detailed studies of the lives of the kings—which included learning by heart their pompous titles, their genealogical tree, and everything about them from their childhood measles to their numerous medals, bestowed by other kings simply for parasitism. Today, schools teach the history of the masses, the class struggle and the objectives and causes of the Revolution.

Marx urged constant "education of the educators." That is what the new Ethiopia is doing, and not only in the classroom. Thousands of future teachers are going to the countryside with their own teachers, who are, at the time, reeducated in the best possible pedagogy: life and the mass struggle.

As part of that singular army of volunteers, they carry out a "campaign" involving enormous efforts to foster the peasant cooperatives and associations; to create mass consciousness in those whom the church and ruling classes inculcated with the belief that God wanted them to suffer on earth in order to gain a passport to heaven; to teach children and adults to read and write; to build dams and roads; and, finally, to contribute to the peasantry's military organization.

The Amharic name for the "campaign" is *zemecha*, and now *zemecha* has gained general respect. Many of its participants have died (as Conrado Benítez died in Cuba), murdered by counterrevolutionaries who can't bear the thought that the masses are being taught.

Ethiopia is also revising where it sends its scholarship students for study abroad. Now they will go not only to imperialist countries, as was the case under the Emperor, but to socialist countries, as well. Before, only a few went to those countries, because there wasn't any interest in having young people know about advanced social systems. Haile Selassie didn't want anything but intellectual slaves.

The Ethiopian Revolution also immediately started organizing the people on the neighborhood level. Associations called *kebele* were created as a first step toward achieving self-government. By September 1977 more than 2,000 of them had been established in the cities and some 600 in rural towns. The average size of a *kebele* ranges from 3,000 to 5,000 families.

In October 1976 democratic elections were held, so the masses could choose their own leaders.

According to their laws, they elect at least 15 members to local leadership, at least 26 to regional leadership and 30 to the central leadership.

The capital has an association that includes 291 grassroots and 25 regional *kebele*.

The *kebele* are more like soviets than the Cuban Committees for the Defense of the Revolution. They are bodies of people's power. The Central Committee of the Association, chosen from the lower bodies, appoints the mayors of the most important cities from among its members.

The *kebele*'s responsibilities in activities for the well-being of the people, in defense operations and in the administration of justice are well defined.

A proclamation issued in October 1977—promoted by Mengistu—gave them the power to establish their own courts of justice and defined the scope of those courts and their procedures in civil and criminal cases.

The same proclamation also described very clearly the other organizations of people's democracy: the associations of workers, women and young people.

January 1977 will go down in the history of the development of the Ethiopian workers' class consciousness. That was when the first step was taken, the founding of the All-Ethiopian Trade Union. The second, culminating step, will be the formation of the Marxist-Leninist Party so the proletariat can carry out its great tasks in alliance with the revolutionary peasantry.

A month later, the factory militias appeared, and, after three weeks of preparation, their members went directly to the battle fronts. Thus, a tradition of workers' resistance—at times intuitive—was continued.

It is true that there had been a trade union organization, the CELU, since 1962, but its action was limited by the fact that it had to coexist with a reactionary government that tried in every possible way—particularly through the relations imposed by the US

AFL-CIO and the ICFTU—to make them trade unions without class content, its leaders, at best, beggars for crumbs, willing to lull the workers' spirit of rebellion.

Now the young, free, trade union movement has its own schools, that teach socialism—which has become the ideal and goal of the entire Ethiopian workers' movement.

Lenin's thesis that, in a revolutionary period, the masses learn in days what it would take them years of normal struggle to learn, is clearly evident in Ethiopia!

From the spontaneous strikes of February 1974, the workers have gone on to protect the factories and enterprises that have been nationalized; to become directly involved in economic activity, with all the difficulties and errors this implies; and to form trade unions as living schools for communism, the ideology of the revolutionary proletariat. Finally, the proletariat has reached the point of creating its own militias and priding itself on its heroism in battle.

There is a well-defined correlation in Ethiopia between the process of socializing the basic means of production and the penetration of socialist ideas in the consciousness of the working masses; although there, too, a phenomenon common to all revolutions has arisen: economism, the eagerness of certain sectors to achieve higher salaries and better living conditions without waiting until the country's economic development permits it. Trotskyite elements fan this negative phenomenon, just as they try to take over the leadership posts in the *kebele* in order to use them, at some point, against revolutionary power. These Trotskyites are firmly rejected by the working masses, but the harm they can do should not be underestimated.

At the beginning of 1975 the banks, the insurance companies, and a total of 65 big enterprises in light industry, the food industry and transportation were nationalized. These were the only industries the country, a victim of underdevelopment, had.

Revolutionary power's record on behalf of the workers is impressive.

As society took for its use what had been produced with social work, the workers became freer. For the first time, political firings—which, until 1974, had led to the concentration camps or forced labor in the Emperor's gold mines—were ended, and wages were set at a level which, while still low, is at least above starvation. In December 1975 came the Labor Proclamation, which caused the old workers to heave a deep sigh of relief. It established books listing the number of workers, enterprise by enterprise, to avoid the situation of "I don't know you, so get out," as well as precise and detailed job descriptions, pay adjustments and working hours.

For the first time, as well, the 8-hour day and 40-hour week, with overtime for extra hours, was approved. And what about the paid vacations, ranging from two weeks to thirty-five days, depending on years of service? Or the full payment for a month's illness—the first month—partial payment for the two succeeding months, and no pay, but the right to return to work, if the illness continues for a longer period?

In an Ethiopia where being a worker used to mean being nobody, the workers now elect representatives to the administrations of the nationalized enterprises and must be consulted and heard in disputes with the many private bosses who still exist in minor branches of the economy.

Slogans reflecting the great change that has taken place are visible on the walls of factories in Addis Ababa: "Fight while producing, produce while fighting" and "Everything for the front! Everything for victory!"

An equally complete transformation has been wrought in the status of the Ethiopian woman.

When you think of what she was like before the Revolution, the word "slave" would be applied not as an adjective but as a noun, in the fullest sense of the word.

In the countryside, the woman had to carry the water, cut the firewood and carry incredible weights on her back and head for many kilometers every day. As the anthropologist R. Forbes has noted, there "Each type of work is exclusively masculine or feminine. There is nothing like it in any other part of the world." She gives this example:

> No male, even at death's door, could take the grain and grind it between the huge rocks used by his mother or wife. The woman prepares all food and drink, but she wouldn't dream of killing even the smallest bird or beast for the kitchen. ... Throughout Ethiopia's changing fortunes, the peasant woman always retained the same anomalous position of flesh for the brothel, with no rights to anything except overwork and undernourishment.
>
> At the very bottom of the social pyramid that rose higher than the Ethiopian mountain peaks, crushed by everyone for every purpose at every moment, the Ethiopian woman was forced to suffer under the cruelest male chauvinism. Her husband frequently sold her, exchanged her or gave her away.
>
> All the evil that the feudal lord visited on the male slave, he in turn visited on the woman.

Is it surprising, then, that the women's associations should be what they are? That they are fully devoted to the Revolution that liberates them completely?

Naturally, many women have become members of the militia and participate actively in the detachments.

The people tell of a number of cases of women who, after nursing their small children, have seized the heights around Dire Dawa from the enemy at bayonet point.

As for the Ethiopian young people, their fervor is everything their age and hopes imply, and their organization is also steadily advancing.

7 Objectives of the Revolution

I

THE SIGNIFICANCE of Haile Selassie's fall from power might be better understood if seen, for a moment, through the eyes of the same aristocracy he so eminently represented, in the lament of an individual such as "King" Simeon of . . . Bulgaria! He is one of those mummies who isn't ashamed to present himself as the monarch of a country that went through not only the republican period but also a revolution, some time ago, after the defeat of fascism. In an article in Madrid's *ABC*, this "king" writes:

> There are times when we can't remain comfortably silent. I'm referring to the situation in Ethiopia, a legendary country, the only one with a millennial history, easily attested to by its many monuments of Black Africa. Who hasn't read about the Queen of Sheba and King Solomon? Or the mysterious Prester John—of the 12th century—or Portugal's influence in Gondar, or the strange and silent obelisks of Axum, sadesert plain of Danakil, lower than the level of These monasteries tell us of the eight centuries during which the church of Abyssinia remained separated from the rest of Christianity. . . . Eight centuries in Africa gave this church its *sui generis* characteristic: its strength for having struggled against paganism in the south and Islam in the north and its archaism, the result of its having been unable to evolve with the rest of the Christian world. The Coptics are Mono-

physites. For them, Christ has only one nature—
the divine—a belief condemned as heresy in the
Council of Calcedonia in 451.

This uniqueness is also characteristic of the
passing of various cultures, reflected in the geography of this great country. . . . From the
legendary mountains of the north, with their
4,900-meter-high peak of Ras Dashan, where
Emperor Theodore decided to be crowned Emperor of the world in the mid-19th century, to the
desert plain of Danakil, lower than the level of
the torrid Red Sea, and from the fertile valleys of
the southwest through virgin forests to the des-
erts of the east, it is a robust, legendary, poor,
glorious, rich, sad, wise, savage, ancient country. . . .

When we think of Ethiopia, its foremost figure,
the protagonist of it all and a personality pro-
jected far beyond that country's extensive
boundaries, we see a man physically small but
spiritually as great as his titles. The King of
Kings, 225th Emperor since the Queen of Sheba,
Lion of Judah and God's Elected, who, as the
head of the church like the Russian Czars, took
the name Haile Selassie—which in Amharic
means Strength of the Trinity—when he as-
cended to the throne.

The provoked fall of a monarch, especially if it
is unjust, may sadden me—because of our af-
finity of position, some readers might justly
say—but what astounds me and should interest a
greater number of people is the speed with
which it occurred and how little it took to bring it
about.

II

The fall of Haile Selassie was just the beginning of
the beginning of the Revolution, a Revolution in
search of its own course.

April 20, 1976, marked a qualitative leap in the
Revolution's level of consciousness and that of all its

people: the adoption and enthusiastic popular approval—in meetings of anywhere from a few to almost a million people—of the Program of the National Democratic Revolution.

That Program can be summed up in two main objectives:

1. establishment of the People's Democratic Republic of Ethiopia and
2. construction of a socialist society, free of the system of man's exploitation of man, and free as well of the oppression of nationalities and antagonisms among them.

To achieve both objectives—so meaningful for the future and always involving difficulties, though much more so in a country such as Ethiopia, whose present was the rest of the world's past—the Ethiopian revolutionary leaders, headed by Mengistu, are working to bring together all genuinely democratic, antifeudal and anti-imperialist forces in a single united front, based on the above Program, and to fuse all the organizationally dispersed Marxist-Leninists in a proletarian Marxist-Leninist Party.

Since February 1974 the forces of the Revolution have been the proletariat, the poor and oppressed peasants, the progressive wing of the petty bourgeoisie—particularly revolutionary students and intellectuals—the military, and other patriotic sectors of the country.

What homage is due the heads of the armed forces who, in spite of their generally petty bourgeois class origins, are doing everything possible to hasten the day when the Party will be the collective leader of the process!

Civilian workers already hold highly responsible posts in the city and the countryside, along with representatives of the radical wing of the military; the presence of these soldiers is in no way militaristic, however, but is rather the guarantee that, despite the errors and complexities inherent in every struggle for a new society that must also be defended at all costs against attack by its internal and external enemies, the advance toward a real and true socialist society continues.

The counterrevolution has also been organizing during this dynamic process, in which everything that had endured for 30 centuries collapsed in just three years.

The counterrevolutionary forces are the toppled feudal lords and bourgeoisie, agents of foreign imperialism—particularly US imperialism—such as the merchant and bureaucratic bourgeoisie. From the very beginning, the reactionary forces of the Arab world have joined the counterrevolutionaries' aggressive strikes.

Prince Fadh, ostensibly the second-ranking official of Saudi Arabia, though first in terms of actual power, has openly declared, "Ethiopia should be carved up and its revolution drowned in blood."

The Prince has conjured up a number of specters (that an independent, revolutionary Ethiopia prevents the Red Sea from being an "Arabian lake," one controlled by the oil-producing reaction; that a popular, strong Ethiopia would aid democratic Yemen, firm bulwark of the revolution in the area; etc.), but the Prince has said more than that to his closest colleagues, and some of them have passed his words along to indiscreet Western journalists: "In our Kingdom, too, we have many potential Mengistus waiting to see what happens to this one. He has to be eliminated so we can go on living in peace."

Anxious to protect their oil route, but, above all, to prevent the triumph of the revolution where the chance of its catching hold seemed so improbable and remote, Arab reaction and imperialism are making plans for direct intervention, which might be hidden behind the proclamation of an Arabian or Muslim republic in Eritrea, which would then ask for foreign aid. At the same time, they are encouraging the two counterrevolutionary parties by financing and arming them. One is the Ethiopian Democratic Union (EDU), the typically fascist spokesman for the latifundists, headed by the prince and heir who was left with the fortune the Emperor had stolen and the desire to succeed him. The other is the Ethiopian Popular Revolutionary Party (EPRP), made up of members of the right wing of the petty bourgeoisie.

The EDU wages war against the peasants from Sudan.

The EPRP specializes in urban assassination attempts.

One enemy tactic has been to provoke numerous right wing coups d'etat—which fortunately, have been put down.

Ethiopia has not been Africa's Chile, but it is prepared to be its Vietnam, Mengistu has said.

III

The National Democratic Program of the Revolution faces truly extraordinary difficulties, objective and subjective, that threaten not only its aims but even the existence of revolutionary power.

Although the economists who study Africa, Ethiopian economists among them, are accustomed to describing what existed there up to 1974 as an economically backward feudal-bourgeois system, this is really a very general way to put it, according to Mengistu. Feudal forms were really predominant; capitalism had scarcely appeared, and, where it did exist, it was deformed. The country was really much more backward than the rest of Africa.

In 1974, agriculture was so bound to the most rigid feudal practices that its surplus production almost never reached the market; it was used to maintain feudal parasites. Even so, it accounted for 50 percent of the country's Gross National Product. The industrial sector contributed only 16 percent, and this industry was confined to small-scale manufacturing and artisan enterprises.

As for the work force, agriculture monopolized 80 percent of the workers, while the incipient industrial sector accounted for less than 8 percent. Low productivity was characteristic of both sectors.

Thus, even though Ethiopia was an agricultural country, with 85 percent of the population living in the countryside and with tremendous natural resources, the Ethiopian people usually went to bed hungry, and every drought brought long periods of famine. It couldn't have been otherwise, for the country wasn't even self-sufficient in the most basic foodstuffs. The growth rate in agriculture was constantly below that of the populations.

Foreign trade also reflected this situation. Agriculture accounted for 90 percent of total exports, while industry didn't even come up to 5 percent.

Because most industries were owned by foreigners and produced consumer goods (it was unthinkable to have even one factory that produced means of production), and because these industries had no relationship to the country's agricultural base, they depended entirely on raw materials and semifinished goods that had to be bought abroad. Thus, foreign debt was as inevitable as famine.

Haile Selassie liked to pretend to tourists and representatives of the various international organizations whose headquarters were in Addis Ababa that the population wasn't hungry and that the poverty wasn't as pervasive as it really was. Therefore, consumer goods were available in the urban shops. Of course, only the aristocrats and the well-paid civilian and military bureaucrats could afford to buy anything in those stores.

The same depressing characteristics pervaded every facet of life.

There were only 3 kilometers of roads for every

10,000 people, and 7 kilometers of passable routes for every 1,000 square kilometers of land.

You can imagine the situation in the social services, health, education and housing. Fidel told the world, "Imperialism and neocolonialism left in Ethiopia—I repeat this because we have to learn these figures by heart—150,000 people with leprosy, 450,000 with tuberculosis, 6 or 7 million with malaria and 14 million with eye infections; 90 percent illiteracy and undernourishment. That's what imperialism and neocolonialism left in Ethiopia! Plus 125 doctors, who, for the most part, were trained in foreign universities and lived in the capital. As is frequently the case in Africa and in underdeveloped countries in other parts of the world, nobody could make them move one kilometer out of the capital."

Even under the best of circumstances—with domestic peace (which is impossible after a revolution) and the affected international monopolies taking a positive position and even helping out—it would have been very difficult for a country such as Ethiopia to overcome all that.

It has to be all uphill for a people who must confront such backwardness, poverty and underdevelopment in the midst of a civil war provoked by the latifundists in the countryside and imperialism's terrorists in the cities, in addition to fighting on four of its borders and throughout its largest regions!

Industry was nationalized in Ethiopia because it had served a few privileged people. If this step—along with that of nationalizing the land and allowing the peasants to work it for their own benefit—hadn't been taken, the Revolution would have resulted in the toppling of a crown, but not in the rising of a people.

Nevertheless, many of those factories have had to close down, because the imperialists have imposed the same kind of blockade the United States imposed on Cuba: refusing to sell raw materials and spare parts; pulling out technicians; and, through the CIA, engaging in sabotage pure and simple—including the use of dynamite.

In the countryside, the latifundists have tried everything: recruiting mercenaries to burn warehouses, homes and the crops in the fields; pushing slander campaigns; and printing counterfeit money in order to instill lasting suspicion in the new trade relations between the peasants' associations and the urban warehouse organizations that can no longer be supplied with imported canned goods.

The agrarian reform in Ethiopia is justified, first of all, on the basis of its great achievement in wiping out hunger.

At the same time, it has created new needs that have to be satisfied to maintain the enthusiasm of the most backward sectors of the peasant masses. Naturally, the peasants are interested in having shoes and other clothing, sugar, matches and even certain household goods. Historically, these desires are positive, because they create a market for expanded production and contribute to breaking through the "natural" feudal economy of producing for consumption rather than for sale.

The violent shattering of social structures occurred before the right conditions had been created for building new structures. As the head of the Cuban Revolution has pointed out many times, imperialism and capitalism couldn't afford to train workers and peasants as technicians and administrators who could manage things for themselves and build a socialist system. Far less so could feudalism!

Ethiopia is, therefore, being run by people who must fight to defend their country while at the same time learning how to administer it, how to direct its economy, how to efficiently set in motion a productive apparatus.

Concentrating on its own defense, and conscious that a counterrevolutionary victory would subject the country to a bloodbath (the vengeance of the former exploiting classes can be gauged by their never-ending crimes today), the Revolution hasn't been able to put into operation all the measures it would like to use to stimulate the economy and the social services. Instead, it has had to assign food, medicine and transportation to the front. This has been one of the greatest proofs of mass revolutionary patriotism. Not only do the people accept these sacrifices, but the struggle to overcome them involves men, women, veterans who fought against the invader once before, and barefoot children—people who take up their posts with the same fervor with which they work the land that is now theirs and who, once they run out of shells, go on, knife in hand, to attack the enemy's machine-gun nests.

None of the negative aspects of the situation have dampened hopes.

Ethiopia's greatest wealth, now completely its own, is its masses. Fortunately, the country also has many natural resources. Three harvests a year are possible in most places. Its many lakes and rivers abound with fish and birds. Underground resources (oil, natural gas, such precious metals as gold and platinum and other products) are also plentiful.

In 1965, Ethiopia produced 246 million kilowatt-hours of electricity. In 1974, the country was already producing 684 million, 70 percent of which came from hydraulic sources.

At the same time, naturally, per capita use of electricity was one of the lowest in the world: 18 kilowatts. Only 35 percent of current capacity is utilized, because of problems that have paralyzed most of the existing industry. Only 7 percent of the population has access to electricity, and it is almost unheard-of in the countryside.

Ethiopia's admirable efforts in the area of defense are matched by its efforts in the economic field. Its economists are studying, with revolutionary optimism, how to plan, receiving cooperation from the

Soviet Union and other socialist countries. The future
builders of the new society are also being trained in
those countries.

8 Motor of the Revolution

I

SEPTEMBER 12, 1977: I am looking at the crowds that have turned out in the streets of Addis Ababa.

Cuban eyes have seen many social changes, and there isn't much that should surprise them, but the word surprise will do here for lack of a better one. . . . This parade is the mirror of an Ethiopia that, more than being simply new, would have been unimaginable just three years ago. All of it! It's as if we were to say that, three years from now, in 1980, there would be socialism in the United States and a parade like this one. Inconceivable!

No description could do justice to the great parade in this other Revolution Square, and it isn't necessary to set down every detail. These are only brief impressions. . . .

Elementary school students lead the parade, some of them still lacking the standard blue uniform and others without shoes, but all winning everyone's applause as they march in military formation, their arms extended as if holding guns, then breaking ranks for a dance we're told is typical of the southern villages.

The thousands of schoolchildren, lined up in ranks, do something we attribute to their age but later realize is the special touch throughout the parade: after their military maneuvers and their dancing, they suddenly run up to the presidential dais.

The taxi drivers, identifiable by the cars that precede and follow their march, carry all kinds of cloth banners bearing the most combative slogans. You can't help thinking that perhaps they were the very ones who, three years ago, sparked the disintegration of the empire.

Each of the trade unions has a float symbolizing its work, and each also has its own dance group, something like in our carnivals, and all of them wind up with that characteristic race up to the center dais and then away. Later we became aware that the eight-hour parade would have been twice as long without that finale, since, for every spectator seated in the Square, there were more than a hundred people parading—in spite of the climate. At 10:00 A.M., there's biting cold from the mountains; at 1:00 P.M., a penetrating sun that would peel the skin off those who came without a hat or cap; around 5:00 P.M., rain and wind, both of them so strong that the diplomatic corps was unable to march up and greet the members of the PMAC and leaders of the country's two religions, Coptic and Muslim, all seated in the very center of that human sea that, throughout those eight hours, only stopped moving and roaring once—to listen in silence to Mengistu's 45-minute speech, delivered just after the event started and before the parade began to move.

Their agitation became delirious in the presence of the veterans of the campaign against Italy, backs now bent with age, their chests laden with medals, some with wooden lances and lions' skins on their heads (presented to exceptional warriors by the best hunters, who also have a right to wear them) and many brandishing swords taller than themselves, with which they pounded the ground as if in a state of ecstasy, delivering fiery harangues against the new invaders. It must be said that these old warriors occasionally flung themselves at Mengistu without his personal bodyguards' flickering an eyelash; in fact, the guards were nearly forced to go with them to where the rest of the comrades were frenetically dancing and yelling. . . .

There were trucks decorated to depict current events. One of them showed the literacy campaign, with a child teaching an old man how to read. Another, representing the plotting of imperialism and Arab reaction, had a very fat man, in a frock coat with a dollar sign on his back, and a very fat veiled lady with a half moon on her head. Together, they pushed a huge wooden saw across a cloth map of Ethiopia until it split apart in the center and armed militia members burst forth, waving the national flag. Another truck showed the planting and picking of coffee. . . .

The high point came when, in a downpour, the peasant militias, including some all-women units, began to march past in their camouflage uniforms, followed by the recently formed workers' militias dressed in gray tweed. The bad weather in no way dampened their martial gait, mastered in just three weeks. More bothersome were the boots worn by those accustomed to walking barefoot, sometimes even preferring to go into battle that way. The wind beat furiously against the huge pictures of Marx, Engels and Lenin but failed to dislodge them from their posts of honor, while the militia members turned their faces toward them and saluted the head of the Revolution as he stood on the dais. . . . A high-ranking PMAC official told me why everyone applauded so loudly and continuously: from Revolution Square they would march directly to the battle front. Swinging along at double time, they reached the trucks that awaited them a hundred meters farther on, their drivers already at the wheel.

II

This is Ethiopia today.

This is how you might picture it, comparing the country's leap into the void left on September 12, 1974, by the passage through its bloody scene of an anti-humanity man, and the parade this past September 12,

1977, of an entire humanized people. Will it fall into the abyss, perish or reach the other side?

The world is now so revolutionary that such leaps are possible, but it's not so revolutionary that victory can be assured in advance.

The motor, or the struggle, will determine the result.

Various forces are fused in that motor. First, the heroism of the Ethiopian masses, who, in addition to ridding the country of the farcical and cruel demigod who occupied it, also discovered the greatest of all history's secrets: their own role. Then came the unity of the revolutionary groups and the wisdom of the leaders of these masses, whose "giant stride" can no longer be stopped. And, finally, the encouragement of the masses elsewhere in the world. Wherever they have a voice, support is shown through the position their state takes and by the action of those governments that cannot ignore them.

The countries of Africa and of the rest of the "Third World" have a special responsibility.

If Ethiopia does not collapse and fall into the abyss opened by its enemies—the traffickers in oil, arms, gold and blood—if it succeeds in reaching its goal, the children of this vast forgotten world will have leaped ahead at least two generations.

Ethiopia's leap leaves behind feudalism, neo-colonialism and capitalism, and also says: "If Ethiopia could do it, everyone can."

This is the time, then, to feed the motor.

It is fitting here to recall the beautiful, passionate words of Karl Marx at a meeting of the International Working Men's Association held in The Hague in 1872. He said, "Citizens, let us think of the fundamental principal of the International, solidarity! It is by establishing this vivifying principle on a strong basis among all the working people of all countries, that we shall achieve the great goal we have set ourselves."

9 Diary of the Revolution

1974

February 13, 1974   Gasoline prices increased.

February 18, 1974   Ethiopian teachers and taxi drivers went on strike.

February 20, 1974   Students and workers in a peaceful demonstration in Addis Ababa against the government; made political demands for the first time.

February 23, 1974   The government was forced to roll back the gasoline price increase. Opposition gained momentum when it became apparent that the government had cheated them to justify its gasoline price increase.

February 27, 1974   The feudal, oligarchial Cabinet of Akilou Habte-Wolde was toppled by popular pressure.

February 28, 1974   The feudalistic government put on a new mask with the appointment of Endalkatchew Makonnen as Prime Minister.

March 25, 1974   The Commission of Enquiry legally established to investigate alleged misuse of public funds and property, unlawful enrichment and maladministration of justice.

April 26, 1974   Members of the former Cabinet detained.

June 28, 1974   A Coordinating Committee of the Armed Forces, Police and Territorial Army was established to work with the new Cabinet.

July 4, 1974   Dejazmatch Tsehayu Enko-Selassie,

Chief Administrator of Kaffa Province under the Haile Selassie regime, killed in Selale region after refusing to surrender to the Coordinating Committee of the Armed Forces and to the Ethiopian people.

July 6, 1974 The Coordinating Committee ordered former officials to hand over government property, and secured amnesty for political prisoners and refugees.

July 8, 1974 The Coordinating Committee issued a statement containing 13 points explaining the aims and objectives of "Ethiopia Tikdem"—Ethiopia First.

July 9, 1974 Ethiopian political refugees invited to return home from abroad.

July 22, 1974 The Cabinet of Endalkatchew Makonnen dissolved, and, as demanded by the Coordinating Committee, Lij Mikael Imru became Prime Minister.

August 16, 1974 The Coordinating Committee abolished the feudal Crown Council; the Imperial "Chilot," which used to review court cases appealed to the former Emperor; and the "Chilot" Judicial Review Commission.

August 22, 1974 A freeze on house and shop rents announced.

August 24, 1974 Administrators and officials of the "Bejirond Office" (Treasury) forbidden to authorize withdrawal of public money without the approval of the Ministry of Finance.

August 25, 1974 The National Resources Development Share Company transferred to public ownership.

August 27, 1974 The Anbassa Bus Transport Company transferred to public ownership.

August 31, 1974 Government financing for training abroad is henceforth to be granted on a competitive merit basis.

September 5, 1974 The St. George Brewery and the

Haile Selassie Prize Trust transferred to the Ministry of Finance. (The former Emperor had earned more than $11 million in dividends from the brewery.)

September 11, 1974   Institutions run by the Welfare Trust came under government supervision— five hospitals, three clinics, two orphanages, two homes for the aged, hotels, buildings and agricultural estates. It was disclosed that the former Emperor was unwilling to bring back to the country fortunes he had amassed in foreign banks.

September 12, 1974   Haile Selassie was deposed. The 1955 Constitution, which gave complete power to the Emperor, was suspended. Parliament, established on feudal and nobility class lines, dissolved.

Guidelines for Ethiopia's new foreign policy issued.

September 15, 1974   The Provisional Military Administrative Council assumed the functions of head of state; the duties and functions of the PMAC's President were made public.

September 22, 1974   Establishment of a Civilian Advisory Body to work closely with the Provisional Military Government.

October 4, 1974   Import of luxury cars forbidden.

October 5, 1974   Members of the aristocracy and former officials ordered to pay tax arrears on urban houses and vast rural farmlands.

October 17, 1974   Municipal Councils abolished.

October 18, 1974   Establishment of *Zemecha,* the National Work Campaign for Development through Cooperation, announced.

October 19, 1974   Establishment of Special General and District Courts-Martial to try former officials for alleged corruption, maladministration and unlawful enrichment.

November 4, 1974   Government buildings, cars and

villas illegally given to members of the aristocracy and officials transferred back to the government.

November 13, 1974   Commission of Enquiry disclosed names of officials against whom criminal proceedings should be brought for breach of
official duties in connection with the disastrous
famine in Wollo Province.

November 23, 1974   Lt. Gen. Aman Mickael Andom
relieved as President of the PMAC.

November 24, 1974   Lt. Gen. Aman Mickael Andom
and other officers executed for attempting to
divide members of the Armed Forces, and
provoking bloodshed in the country.

November 28, 1974   Brig. Gen Teferi Bante appointed
President of the PMAC.

November 30 — December 2, 1974   The PMAC took
measures to protect public safety and served
stern warning against criminal elements following bomb explosions at Municipality of
Addis Ababa and Wabe Shebelle Hotel and at
Bole Airport.

December 13, 1974   A delegation of the International
Committee of the Red Cross issued a statement
saying that it was impressed with the treatment
of detained former officials.

December 20, 1974   The Provisional Military Government declared policy guidelines on Ethiopian socialism, stating that the common good
takes precedence over the pursuit of individual
gains.

Resources that are either crucial for economic
development or are of such character that they
provide an indispensable service to the community are to be brought under government control.

Strengthening of cultural development on the
basis of equality among various ethnic groups
in the country.

The right to self-administration and popular participation of the people without foreign interference in the country's internal affairs.

In foreign policy, noninterference in the domestic affairs of independent nations and Ethiopia's readiness to promote the advancement of African development and freedom were stressed.

December 21, 1974   National Work Campaign for Development through Cooperation launched throughout the country.

December 23, 1974   Public holidays designated without religious bias.

December 27, 1974   Radio Ethiopia for the first time began nationwide broadcasts in the Oromo language.

1975

January 1, 1975   Three commercial banks, three other financial institutions and 14 insurance companies transferred to public ownership.

January 4, 1975   The Provisional Military Government issued a statement on efforts to find a peaceful solution to the Eritrean problem.

February 3, 1975   Seventy-two privately owned industrial and commercial companies brought under government control.

February 4, 1975   Amnesty announced for persons in hiding for crimes committed during the former regime.

February 8, 1975   Visiting members of Amnesty International briefed on the set-up and procedures of the Special General Court-Martial trying former officials. They also attended a session of the Court.

February 15, 1975   State of emergency declared in Eritrea administrative region to ensure public safety and maintain law and order.

February 16, 1975   Mass demonstrations in Addis Ababa condemn perpetrators of disorder and counterrevolutionary acts in Eritrea.

February 17, 1975   New national emblem to reflect the spirit of Ethiopian socialism while maintaining the historical heritage of Ethiopia.

March 4, 1975   All rural land in Ethiopia proclaimed the collective property of the people, thus putting an end to the feudal system of land tenure.

March 5, 1975   Close to 800,000 persons in Addis Ababa in mass rally supporting nationalization of all rural land.

Temporary surtax introduced to raise more funds for drought relief and rehabilitation.

March 21, 1975   Asfa Wossen's appointment as king-designate annulled; all royal titles abolished.

April 6, 1975   For the first time, the actual Victory Day marking the end of the 1936–41 Italian fascist occupation of Ethiopia was observed throughout the country. May 5 used to be observed, to glorify the day the former Emperor returned to Addis Ababa from exile.

May 1, 1975   May Day was officially observed for the first time in Ethiopia.

May 8, 1975   A deputation of the Afar people explained their sufferings under the feudal regime to the PMAC's President and Vice-President, who, in turn, briefed the Afar people's representatives on the policies of the new government.

May 16, 1975   Private aircraft companies and all light aircraft in the country and a number of supermarkets in Addis Ababa belonging to expatriates transferred to public ownership.

May 24, 1975   Science and Technology Commission established.

July 26, 1975   All land and "surplus houses" in urban centers throughout the country were nationalized effective August 7, 1975.

September 29, 1975   Private schools brought under government control.

December 6, 1975   New labor law proclaimed.

December 13, 1975   A proclamation strengthening the farmers' associations was announced.

December 29, 1975   Proclamation regulating private capital announced.

1976

January 3, 1976   Tax on the use of land and agricultural produce proclaimed.

April 20, 1976   The Program of the National Democratic Revolution was announced. Proclamation establishing the Provisional Office for Mass Organization Affairs.

May 16, 1976   A 9-point policy declaration on peacefully solving the Eritrean problem announced. The Yekatit School of Ideology established.

July 7, 1976   Special Commission dealing with affairs in the Administrative Region of Eritrea established.

July 17, 1976   Nationwide celebrations marking the end of the first phase of the National Work Campaign—*Zemecha*—observed.

August 21, 1976   Two hundred and nine political prisoners who had been under detention pardoned and released.

September 23, 1976   An attempt made to assassinate Comrade Lt. Col. Mengistu Haile Mariam, President of the PMAC.

October 9, 1976   A proclamation for the consolidation and organization of urban dwellers' associations and reform of the organizational set-up of municipalities issued; it defines the duties and functions of the *kebele*, higher and central associations and the interrelations among them.

November 26, 1976   A proclamation establishing a Road Transport Authority was issued.

1977

January 13, 1977   A proclamation establishing a Higher Education Commission and specifying the objectives of higher education in the country issued.

February 3, 1977   The Provisional Military Administrative Council foiled an attempted counter-revolutionary coup against it. The counter-revolutionaries, Brig. Gen. Teferi Bante, Lt. Col. Asrat Desta, Lt. Col. Hiruy Haile Selassie, Captain Mogus Wolde-Michael, Captain Teferra Deneke, Captain Alemayehu Haile and Corporal Hailu Belay, were executed the same day.

February 11, 1977   A newly revised proclamation defining the powers and responsibilities of the PMAC and the Council of Ministers issued. In line with the provisions of the proclamation, Comrade Lt. Col. Mengistu Haile Mariam appointed President of the PMAC, and Comrade Lt. Col. Atnafu Abate, Vice-President.

March 14, 1977   Fidel Castro arrived in Addis Ababa on a three-day visit to Ethiopia.

April 12, 1977   Comrade Lt. Col. Mengistu Haile Mariam, President of the PMAC, addressed the Call of the Motherland to the nation, urging the Ethiopian people to defend the unity and territorial integrity of the country, now being violated by foreign invading forces in the north and the east.

April 14, 1977   Nearly half a million people gathered at Revolution Square to demonstrate their anger at foreign armed intervention in Ethiopia and to declare their determination to safeguard their Revolution, unity and territorial integrity.

April 21, 1977   The Revolutionary Administration and Development Committees were replaced by Revolution and Development Committees with broad mandates to help expedite the progress of the ongoing Revolution in urban and rural areas.

April 23, 1977 Four American organizations in Addis Ababa—the Kagnew Station, Military Assistance Advisory Group, Naval Medical Research Unit, United States Information Service—closed down by order of the Ethiopian government. The foreign staffs of the organizations ordered to leave the country within a week's time.

May 3, 1977 Comrade Lt. Col. Mengistu Haile Mariam left on an official and friendly five-day visit to the Soviet Union, at the invitation of the Government and Communist Party of the USSR.

May 28, 1977 The Defense Attachés' offices of the United States, Egypt and Britain closed.

Two thirds of the Marine guards of the US Embassy also ordered to leave the country. The United States Embassy instructed to reduce its diplomatic staff by half.

June 25, 1977 Ethiopia's 300,000-strong People's Militia was launched at a mammoth parade in Addis Ababa, in which 100,000 representatives of the Armed Forces and the People's Militia participated. The parade was watched by half a million people.

July 14, 1977 A proclamation defined the relations between the Standing Committee of the PMAC with the POMOA and the Political School.

August 20, 1977 Comrade Lt. Col. Mengistu Haile Mariam, PMAC President, made a call for general mobilization to the Ethiopian people.

August 24, 1977 A mammoth mass rally was held in Addis Ababa in support of the total mobilization call addressed to the people.

August 27, 1977 The National Revolutionary Operations Command (NROC), with five sector commands in the north, south, east and west established.

September 12, 1977 Parade for the third anniversary of the Revolution. A million Ethiopians—workers, students, soldiers and workers' and peasants' militias—participate.

About the Author

CURRENTLY a member of the Secretariat of the Central Committee of the Communist Party of Cuba, in charge of foreign affairs for the Party, Raúl Valdés Vivó, born in 1929, has had a truly protean career as novelist, poet, journalist and diplomat. "Revolutionary" is the qualifying word for him in each of these fields. As a youth he was imprisoned for his editorship, underground during the Batista dictatorship, of the magazine *Mella*. He led the Communist students at the University of Havana. When the revolution triumphed in 1959 he became an assistant editor of *Hoy*. Between 1967 and 1974, he served in a succession of diplomatic posts, including the ambassadorship to the then Kingdom of Cambodia; to the NLF and the Provisional Revolutionary Government of South Vietnam (in their jungle headquarters); and, finally, to the Democratic Republic of Vietnam.

As an author he has written two novels, *The Blind Blacks* and *The Brigade and the Maimed Man*. His other works include: *Angola: An End to the Mercenaries Myth, Stories from South Vietnam, Embassy in the Jungle and Before: the 17th Parallel, 12 Vietnamese Short Stories;* a play—*Oranges in Saigon;* and many poems which have appeared in various books and periodicals.

ETHIOPIA'S REVOLUTION

RAÚL VALDÉS VIVÓ

For centuries the broad masses of Ethiopia have fought a bitter, protracted struggle against the colonialists, arrogant invaders and racist powers to defend themselves against these anti-people and anti-peace forces. This long history of struggle of the Ethiopian masses furnishes firm and dependable foundations for the present Democratic Revolution. . . . Our program of the Ethiopian National Democratic Revolution, which is our guide, clearly explains that by abolishing exploitation, oppression, nepotism, bribery, and tribal, religious and sex discrimination we aim to establish a society in which justice, equality and peace prevail. These are prerequisites for the transition to collective progress and at the same time reflect the hopes and aspirations of the oppressed Ethiopian masses.

Lt. Colonel Mengistu Haile Mariam
Chairman of the Provisional Military
Administrative Council

For a complete catalog write

INTERNATIONAL PUBLISHERS
381 Park Avenue South, New York, NY 10016